BEYOND COFFEE

Enjoy the magic!

— JAMES

BEYOND COFFEE

A SUSTAINABLE GUIDE TO NOOTROPICS, ADAPTOGENS, AND MUSHROOMS

JAMES BESHARA WITH DAN ENGLE, MD
AND KATHERINE HAYNES, MPAS, PA-C

MONOCLE
Publishing

BEYOND COFFEE

A Sustainable Guide to Nootropics,
Adaptogens, and Mushrooms

ISBN 978-1-5445-0545-9 *Paperback*

978-1-5445-0546-6 *Ebook*

CONTENTS

The following book provides an overview of various nootropics, adaptogens, herbs, and mushrooms, highlighting their mechanism of action, potential benefits, side effects, and interactions with medications such as blood pressure medication or SSRIs. Many of these compounds have gone through rigorous testing and research, which is discussed here. However, side effects and interactions should be considered for each person on an individual basis. The information presented does not constitute medical advice or recommendations. Please consult your physician about taking any of these compounds, particularly if you have a chronic medical condition or take medications daily, to assure safety.

Visit beyondcoffeebook.com for more information including what the authors take on a daily basis to find their flow-state, interviews, and other resources. You can also use this link to share the first two chapters for free with others.

FOREWORD

In today's technologically activated, ever-increasingly fast-paced digital age, what's the most common medically related focus goal across demographics and ages?

Hands down, it's brain performance.

From Silicon Valley execs to undergraduate and postgraduate students, aging Baby Boomers, military veterans, and at-home digital startup parents, the number one desired area of health, performance, and optimization is the brain.

We are both fascinated and fearful of the future of our immensely magical human brains. On the one hand, gene jockeys promise longer lives. On the other, the epidemic of dementia *en masse* looms in the not-so-distant future. The brain and various approaches to improving cognition are like a neurological Pandora's box. Our brain has the potential to create symphonies of miraculous beauty—as well as degenerate into a puddle of infantile dependency, often in the same lifetime. Thus, the "Decade of the Brain" has brought agents of cognitive performance into the limelight, specifically a novel class of acceleration tools called nootropics.

I first came into contact with a nootropic chemical jet fuel while in my medical training, through a medication that is a close cousin to Ritalin called Cylert. Just before medical school, I broke my neck in a diving accident and suffered my fifth major concussion. While in my psychiatry residency, I got turned upside down in a snowboard park and put a six-inch crack in my helmet, thus receiving my sixth one. These two concussions compounded in effect. I started having severe post-concussive syndrome and narcolepsy, a neurological condition where one gets sudden and uncontrollable sleep attacks. It was beyond miserable.

The only treatment at the time was prescription medication. A chemical rescue pill came into the picture... and it worked! How seductively it worked. Four years into the prescription and it was still working. Then I started experiencing some of its longer-term side effects, like migraine headaches, irritability, and mood swings. I also learned about the likely long-term neurotoxicity of stimulants like these. Plus, I had watched three out of four of my grandparents pass away with neurodegenerative conditions (two from Alzheimer's dementia and one with Parkinson's disease); it was clear there was a need for an integrative, healthier, and more sustainable approach to neurological recovery and longevity.

Little did I know then that this experience would lead to a lifelong passion for exploring the psychiatric realms of cognitive science and regenerative methods, medicines, and technologies.

I've written books on concussion recovery and have medically directed clinics focused on reparative neurobiology and transformational medicine. My medical and experiential background in this space has taught me a few simultaneously simple and profound things:

1. We are each designed to express our unique brilliance.
2. The brain is an infinitely complex, ever-evolving matrix of magic.
3. Everything can be healed and optimized.
4. It's up to each of us to do our due diligence to explore the available options, try them out for individual response, and use them responsibly.

Unbeknownst to me at the time, my brush with an unsustainable neurotoxin prescribed as "medicine" would color my research to not just look for results, but also to pay special attention to the sustainable approach to those results.

In this, the most dynamic time in human history, the human and natural collective needs each of us to be switched on to the best versions of ourselves, to who we are and what we're here to do, for the long term.

In service to this vision, we offer this guide to support you along your journey of self-discovery and sustainable optimal performance. You have a unique genius to shine forth. We're excited to see it.

DAN ENGLE, MD

INTRODUCTION

About five years ago, I was diagnosed with a heart condition—an irregular heartbeat termed "atrial fibrillation." I was twenty-six years old. When the doctor told me the diagnosis, he asked me about my lifestyle, habits, stress, and exercise regimens. Then he asked how much caffeine I consumed each day. I told him that it was "anywhere between five and six cups" of coffee. He nodded, barely reacting, as if I had confirmed something in his mind. Then, in a somewhat unsurprised manner, he said that my caffeine consumption was likely the major contributor to developing a condition like atrial fibrillation this early in my life.

He said, "James, with your condition, you really

shouldn't consume more than 80 mg of caffeine a day."

"Okay, how much is that in terms of coffee?" I had no idea what I was about to agree to.

"Well, at five to six cups, you're currently consuming about ten times that amount."

Despite the fact that I had just heard the news that I had a heart condition (one that I didn't know existed prior to that doctor's visit, about which I didn't know the implications nor the severity), I remember being most overwhelmed by my doctor's suggestion that I reduce my caffeine intake to about half a cup of coffee. At that time, I was running a company of 70 employees, and I couldn't imagine taking my energy crutch away. I remember seeing article after article touting how great coffee was for you. I thought about bringing those articles up to my doctor. Then I remembered he was my doctor, not some person who was casually deriding my bitter, black, productivity muse.

Conversationally, we only spent a few more moments on the topic, because there were larger things to discuss (like going to the ER for a cardioversion; fun!). But in our subsequent meetings, in which he continued to make the case for decreasing my caffeine intake, he mentioned green tea (specifically matcha green tea) as a great alternative to coffee. It contained less than 80 mg of caffeine and, he said, "includes another compound called l-theanine that adds a calm focus in addition to the reaction of caffeine...It helps reduce the anxiety that coffee can give you as well."

I can't say it was game-changing at the time. But it did crack the door in my mind to an alternative to coffee. I was intrigued by the comment that another compound, when added to caffeine, could get me closer to what I was ultimately seeking in the first place: short-term and long-term productivity.

I took it for granted that coffee was the ambitious person's best friend. But five years and 40-plus iterations with different compounds later, I have learned about the different compounds from around the world that allow me to consume a fraction of the caffeine I used to, yet produce a multiple of the energy and productivity that coffee once delivered. These compounds include adaptogens, anti-inflammatories, herbs, mushrooms, and brain-focused supplements, sometimes called nootropics.

I experimented, researched, and sought expertise on the good, the bad, and the ugly: the short-term boosts and long-term drains, the shortcuts, sifting through science and pseudoscience. I read research paper after research paper and heard anecdote after anecdote. What I came up with was the scientifically scrutinized, well-documented, natural, and most importantly—sustainable—approach to these compounds.

To be clear—and this is very important—each of us should focus on five areas when it comes to energy, focus, and productivity, in this order: sleep, exercise, diet, stress-management, and then exogenous compounds like the ones we have researched and written about in this book. If you sleep two hours a night, it doesn't matter how much caffeine or l-theanine you consume, your productivity will not be optimal. And study after study shows that exercise improves cognitive performance as well as any cognition-enhancing substance.

Additionally, poor diet and high glucose levels

have been linked to chronic fatigue. Constantly overloading your figurative plate, too, without a thoughtful approach to stress-management, strains your focus and the relationships with those around you. A guide to the sustainable approach to nootropics would not be complete without calling this out.

In addition to talking with your doctor about any of these supplements, herbs, roots, or mushrooms **before taking any of them**, you should also talk to your doctor about establishing goals in these prerequisite four areas as well.

Here are our quick tips on those four other areas before jumping into the rest of the book:

Sleep: Aim for seven to eight hours of sleep each night, while waking up each morning at the same time. Waking up at different times each morning throws off your circadian rhythm and does not allow your body to create a stable, dependable one. No matter what time you go to sleep, try to wake up at the exact same time each morning for optimal sleep each night. Need help falling asleep at an earlier time and don't want to risk tossing about? The second-best piece of advice on this topic I received from the same sleep doctor was to use 300 micrograms (**not** milligrams, as that is too much) of melatonin about three hours before you want to fall asleep to kickstart your natural production of melatonin.

Exercise: Practice 30 mins of aerobic exercise three times per week. Get your heart rate up and get your sweat glands going (your skin is your largest organ, after all, put it to work).

Diet: Everything in moderation. There is a lot of compelling research around intermittent fasting (eating within time boundaries of eight to ten hours each day) to optimize both cognitive function and lifespan.[1]

Stress-Management: Apps like Headspace and Calm can be great for easily creating level-setting habits once a day around meditation. Another trick is to not over-promise or over-commit each day. As the adage goes "everything takes twice as long and is three times more expensive than you think"—so plan accordingly by committing to half the things you think you can accomplish in a day. It will leave you the slack in the day to really knock something out of the park, as well as give you ample space for spontaneity or seizing an opportunistic moment that you wouldn't have otherwise had the time or energy to contemplate. Warren Buffett and his partner Charlie Munger, two of the most famous investors of all time, famously plan four hours each day just for thinking. Plan a few minutes later today just to think about that!

Exogenous compounds (supplements, herbs, mushrooms, and so on—that is, many of the compounds in this book): Avoid addictive, short-term, unsustainable approaches to these compounds. You want scientifically proven effects to build over time in a safe way. It's also simpler to find what works for you for smaller (but more sustainable) gains that build up over time—rather than short bursts of productivity that help you today but make you pay tomorrow (or help you today but are habit-forming and addictive, where the effects actually diminish over time instead of building). Our definition of a "sustainable approach" is one that is (a) safe, (b) scientifically proven to work, (c) beneficial long term, and (d) non-habit forming.

We will discuss some of the most popular nootropics that very clearly DO NOT fit in this category. Nootropics that are either not safe long term, or are addictive and build tolerance over time would not be sustainable in our view. Something that is not proven safe but may be effective would also not fall into our bucket. Many people find benefits from a wide range of nootropics that we don't endorse. This book is not a *Guide to Nootropics* as much as it is a *Sustainable Guide to Nootropics*. We have rated each compound on a "sustainability scale" that is at the intersection of safety, efficacy, and long-term application. We recommend any compound that is at four or five stars, but we do not recommend any compounds that fall below four stars, often because of safety or discontinuation/habit-forming concerns.

SO WHAT ARE NOOTROPICS?

Nootropics, pronounced "new-tropics" (though many people say "new-troh-pics" interchangeably), comes from a Greek origin of 'nous-trepein' which means "mind-bending." The word was coined in the 1970s by the chemist and psychologist Corneliu Giurgea.

The term is increasingly broad, as it is used to define a growing category of compounds that improve cognitive function. Like the term "vitamins," it's a large umbrella of many sub-categories. The more we learn about cognitive performance, the more we learn that in addition to pharmaceutically-created compounds that are created for increasing attention span, or over-the-counter herbs that can increase memory, things like anti-inflammatory compounds (like natural turmeric curcumin) can boost cognition by relieving the brain of inflammation. Instead of adding to the system, they help remove blockers of cognitive performance. Ten years ago, compounds like turmeric curcumin would not have been seen as a typical "nootropic" compound, but the surface area is ever-expanding as more and more individuals and researchers find ways to optimize cognitive performance.

Nootropics therefore include wide varieties of supplements (like CDP-choline), roots (Maca), herbs (bacopa), fungi (lion's mane mushrooms), coffee or teas (like matcha green tea), or drugs (like Adderall). Not all are equal. Not all are safe. Not all are well understood. Not all are meant for long-term consumption. What we felt was missing online or in the research was a guide for the safe, non-habit forming supplements, roots, herbs, and fungi that you can take every day to either improve memory (bacopa monnieri, a natural herb that has shown clinically verified improvements of up to 20 percent), improve focus (alpha-GPC, a natural choline compound has shown clinically verified improvements in cognitive performance in patients taking the compound for 90 days[2]) or improve energy (there are more compounds around the world that give us energy besides caffeine—and they decrease inflammation, a drain of energy for the body).

Before we begin, let's address a few misconceptions.

New compounds are being discovered or purported each year, and the research on newer nootropics is often scant. Serious consequences can come from taking compounds that are poorly understood and poorly researched. However, there is a common misconception that all nootropics are poorly understood. This is not the case. Many compounds, from bacopa monnieri to modafinil are exceptionally well-studied and scientifically researched, with decades of rigorous, double-blind studies confirming and reconfirming their benefits.

Two additional misconceptions about nootropics are that "they are unsafe" or "they don't work." However, that is the equivalent of believing something as vague and uninformed as "supplements are not safe" or "supplements don't work"—some supplements are not safe and some are, some supplements work and others don't. All four of these potential realities are true for nootropics. We intend to guide you through what the research says is and isn't safe and what it says does and doesn't work.

Misconceptions are common with new trends, and they generally come about because something is still early in scientific and cultural discovery. Many of these misconceptions are similar to those two hundred years ago at the beginning of our cultural introduction to coffee, one of the original nootropics, with the concept of coffee houses. We think time will tell that coffee was far from the end of the story. It's much more likely that its discovery was just the beginning.

Lastly, what do we mean by sustainability?

Within this book, we use a "Sustainability Score" of 1-5 stars, with 5 stars being an herb or compound that you can take every day safely and effectively. Some compounds and herbs actually require days or weeks of usage to find the true benefits, and there are others that will give you a short-term boost, say five to eight hours of benefit—but then your productivity falls off a cliff after that. It's robbing Peter to pay Paul.

With our approach, and through a lens of sustainability, we want you to know which compounds have shown clinical benefit from all three vectors of safety, efficacy, and sustained usage. In other words, we believe in consuming compounds where day three is even better than day one, and day 53 is better than both of those. A big reason we put this book together for you is that we were craving this kind of lens when it came to cognition-enhancing supplements ourselves. We hope you find the same benefits we have in our own lives in compiling this research.

NOOTROPICS

CHAPTER ONE

INTRODUCTION TO NOOTROPICS

Wouldn't it be great to be able to take a pill or drink a tea and be smarter? Think of the movie *Limitless*. Simply pop a pill, and suddenly, you can game the stock market like a pro or help the FBI solve a murder mystery. While those may be great premises for fiction, and most people expect nothing more than that, the truth is that there are, in fact, chemical compounds scientifically designed to boost your mental capacity and abilities. And these new supplements are becoming extremely popular.

Called nootropics, these health supplements claim to offer a variety of brain-boosting benefits, including improving memory, focus, energy, and the ability to learn, as well as fueling creativity, sharpening attention span, and boosting the brain's executive functions.

The questions are whether or not they actually work; whether or not they're safe; and how to find that intersection of efficacy and safety. That's the focus of this book.

There is a lot of information available online, in published research, and through speaking with experts; some of it is helpful, some of it isn't. As we thought about how to highlight the best research, compounds, and approaches to cognitive-enhancing supplements, herbs, fungi, roots, and the like, we realized there was a gap in the information. We could find research that showed short-term benefits with X or safety with Y, but we couldn't find a good resource for the safe, effective, comprehensive, and sustainable approach to these compounds. So we set out to write it ourselves. Please let us know what you think at beyondcoffeebook2019@gmail.com, and we will aim to incorporate feedback into future versions of this book.

OVERVIEW AND HISTORY

Despite being a relatively recent health trend, nootropics have been around a lot longer than most of us realize. For example, caffeine and other stimulants that fall into the nootropic category have been in use for centuries.

We haven't always called them by the name "nootropics," however; as the term was coined in 1972 by Romanian psychologist and chemist Corneliu Giurgea, when he developed the compound Piracetam.

Today, a nootropic is any chemical or chemical compound that is designed to improve cognitive functions. A variety of research has gone into determining not only whether nootropics work (more on that below), but also why they work. According to research published by the National Institutes of Health (NIH):

> Nootropics act as a vasodilator against the small arteries and veins in the brain. Introduction of natural nootropics in the system will increase the blood circulation to the brain and at the same time provide the important nutrients, increase energy, and improve oxygen flow to the brain.[1]

Most nootropics can be found in either natural sources or over-the-counter supplements. Some are available only through prescription. Some compounds are created by extracting the chemicals from their naturally occurring sources, while others are synthesized in laboratories.

CHAPTER TWO

POPULAR (AND MOST-RESEARCHED) NOOTROPICS

When it comes to nootropics, it's always a question of if they work and if there are any safety concerns. In terms of if they work, most nootropic users find that they can customize the outcomes by taking a mix of compounds—a cocktail that formulators call "stacks." This is to say that there is no one single pill or compound that will have the entire desired effect; often a mixture of compounds work together to produce results. A wide variety of compounds are available commercially, each with slightly different chemical structures and thus potentially different outcomes. The "does it work" question, then, has to be answered by determining what works for each user on a personal level.

In terms of safety, most nootropics have been laboratory tested, and some have been FDA approved (though not all of them). Anyone looking to experiment with nootropics should be aware of potential side effects and, as stated in the introduction, should consult their doctor before trying these compounds on your own.

> Note: Please be advised that many of these compounds may also interact with other medications (most commonly those for diabetes and high blood pressure). We have included many, but not all, of the common side effects and drug interactions for your reference at the end of this book.

Following is a list of the most commonly used and sought-after nootropics, prioritized by what we view as a positive intersection of safety and efficacy, a brief description of their effects, research conducted on them, and any safety concerns. We have also included a sustainability score of zero to five stars, with zero meaning that even a single dosage of the compound is not worth the potential cognitive benefit—and five stars being a compound that you can take every day and continue to benefit from even after months of continuous use.

Our research should be seen more as a starting point than a final evaluation, since each person may react differently to different nootropics. And we'll say it a third time: anyone considering incorporating nootropics into their daily routine should seek out additional research and consult with a medical professional before embarking on any direct experimentation.

Following the list of nootropics are overviews of some of the most popular adaptogens (de-stressing agents), mushrooms, and anti-inflammatories. Because of the interchangeability of some of these terms, you may see compounds show up in more than one place.

OMEGA-3 EPA AND DHA

Sustainability Score: 5/5 Stars

Omega-3 is the category of fatty acids, most commonly (but not exclusively) derived from fish and are essential for brain and eye health. They are found in high levels in salmon and tuna and must be consumed through diet or supplements (i.e., the body cannot synthesize them). Omega-3 supplements are most commonly taken to help reduce cholesterol and risk of heart disease. However, several studies have also brought omega-3 fatty acids into the arena of cognitive enhancement and improved attention span. The most researched omega-3s are the two most biologically active, DHA (Docosahexaenoic Acid) and EPA (eicosapentaenoic acid). Omega-3s have the rare distinction of being both neuroprotective and neurorehabilitative for those who have experienced traumatic brain injury. If you're like us, you will see studies with *low dosages* that debate the efficacy of omega-3 supplements. However the efficacy of omega-3 supplementation across these various neurological benefits is very clear at physician recommended dosages.

Does it work?

Research shows that those who increase intake of

omega-3s have enhanced cognitive performance. Interestingly, having lower levels of DHA in the blood has been associated with "amyloidosis" (deposits of protein called amyloids on the brain), but having higher levels of DHA in the blood is associated with preserved brain volume.[1] One scientific trial demonstrated that elderly adults experienced improvements in verbal immediate recall after taking DHA linked to phosphatidylserine (PS) for 15 weeks.[2] A larger study on elderly adults followed for almost four years revealed those who regularly ate fish or who supplemented with omega-3 fatty acids (particularly DHA) were less likely to develop Alzheimer's disease.[3] There have also been some large scale reviews looking at the effects of omega-3s on cognitive performance. Based on these reviews we can conclude that those with mild cognitive impairment at baseline do better with omega-3 fatty acid intake. But those with no cognitive impairment at baseline and those already diagnosed with Alzheimer's disease do not appear to benefit.[4][5][6][7] More studies are needed to confirm these conclusions.

Omega-3 fatty acids have also been shown to be beneficial for those with ADHD. A 2018 review of all the literature demonstrated that youth with

ADHD have been found to be deficient in DHA and EPA at baseline, and that supplementation with omega-3 fatty acids decreases ADHD symptoms and improves cognitive performance for these individuals.[8]

And as a bonus, omega-3 fatty acids have been studied extensively, and proven beneficial, in their ability to lower blood pressure and cholesterol levels,[9] and in some people EPA specifically may even decrease symptoms of depression.[10]

Is it safe?

Omega-3 supplements are generally considered safe when taken at the recommended dosage, but consuming too much may result in immune system suppression or an increased risk for bleeding due to impaired clot formation. The FDA recommends dietary supplementation of DHA + EPA combined not to exceed 2g/day.[11]

ALPHA-GPC

Sustainability Score: 5/5 Stars

Similar to CDP choline, alpha-GPC works on the brain to improve memory, cognition, and learning, but packs a bigger punch of choline and is also combined with glycerophosphate. The modern-day diet is felt to be choline deficient, and acetylcholine, a choline derivative, is an essential neurotransmitter in the brain. Like CDP choline, alpha-GPC can be used to treat Alzheimer's and stroke patients. Athletes also often turn to alpha-GPC to aid in growth hormone production and for improved endurance potential.

Does it work?

A handful of studies in both humans and animals have examined the efficacy of alpha-GPC in a variety of populations, and evidence produced so far is promising. An animal study showed that alpha-GPC increases levels of dopamine, an essential neurotransmitter, in the brain.[12] One small clinical study (20 participants) found that acute administration of alpha-GPC did not improve mood, cognition, or athletic performance measured 30 minutes after administration, but this study only measured acute outcomes.[13] Another study found that patients with mild to moderate dementia showed improved cognitive performance after taking alpha-GPC for 90 days.[14] One study also confirmed findings that alpha-GPC can enhance growth hormone production.[15]

Is it safe?

Alpha-GPC is considered "generally recognized as safe" (GRAS) by the FDA.[16] This designation requires multiple layers of safety and testing compliance, including expert panels and rigorous scientific evidence for the safety of a compound within the United States. "Generally Recognized As Safe" status with the Food and Drug Administration is therefore seen as a high distinction of safety in the food, medical, and nutritional spaces, and you will see it listed in various places in this book simply as GRAS.

CDP CHOLINE

Sustainability Score: 5/5 Stars

Also known as citicoline, CDP choline is a chemical that naturally occurs in the body and helps produce the brain chemical phosphatidylcholine, which is needed for the brain to function. As such, citicoline is used to treat Alzheimer's disease, dementia, head trauma, stroke, memory loss, Parkinson's Disease, ADHD, and even glaucoma.

Does it work?

Many animal studies have proven neurocognitive effects of citicoline, including increasing levels of dopamine, noradrenaline, and serotonin in the brain.[17] [18] [19] All available clinical studies were reviewed in 2015 showing conflicting results—while some studies show improvements in cognition for those who supplement with citicoline, others showed no benefit.[20] However a later study on 75 males showed statistically significant improvements in attention, psychomotor speed, and reduced impulsivity for those supplemented with CDP choline compared to placebo.[21] Moreover, a small study of 14 males who took CDP choline after sustaining a concussion showed decreased post-concussive symptoms compared to those who took placebo, suggesting there may be a role for CDP choline for helping the brain recover from injury.[22] It has also been studied for use in treating stroke victims in terms of restoring and repairing their cognitive functions, where evidence suggests CDP choline can be used to reduce lesion volume in the brain.[23]

Is it safe?

CDP Choline, like Alpha-GPC, is considered "generally recognized as safe" (GRAS) by the FDA.[24]

L-THEANINE

Sustainability Score: 5/5 Stars

Also known as theanine, this compound is an amino acid naturally found in a variety of plants and fungi, but most commonly available in green tea. Theanine is thought to have neuroprotective and cognitive-enhancing effects by increasing serotonin, dopamine, GABA, and glycine levels in the brain.[25] [26] As such, it is often used for treating anxiety and high blood pressure, as well as for boosting attention and focus.[27] It is considered most effective when taken in conjunction with caffeine.[28]

Does it work?

Clinical studies on the effects of theanine are promising. One large analysis concluded that theanine taken with caffeine improves alertness and one's accuracy when switching between different tasks.[29] Another study found that theanine improved attention and memory in patients with mild cognitive impairment.[30] Interestingly, theanine has also been shown to improve sleep in those with ADHD or depression.[31] [32] Research remains conflicting regarding theanine and stress reduction. A 2016 review article concluded that theanine can indeed be efficacious in reducing stress and anxiety.[33] One small study of 14 participants concurred with this conclusion, finding that taking theanine prior to an exam may decrease anxiety and prevent blood pressure increases associated with stress.[34] However, another small study with 16 participants concluded that theanine may have a relaxing effect in those already relaxed, but has no effect in a stress-induced state.[35]

Is it safe?

The US FDA has granted theanine Generally Recognized As Safe (GRAS) status, and it is generally considered safe when taken in the short term (up to two months of continuous use).[36] More research is needed on long-term isolated supplementation of theanine, and it is best to avoid if pregnant or nursing. That said, we do know from daily intake of green tea (which includes theanine) that long-term ingestion is well-tolerated and regarded as safe for up to eight cups. More on green tea in Chapter 5.

ASHWAGANDHA

Sustainability Score: 4/5 Stars (not to be taken while pregnant or trying to conceive)

Ashwagandha is a plant, and its roots and berries are used for medicinal purposes. Primarily it is used as an "adaptogen," meaning it is intended to reduce stress levels in the body.

Does it work?

Ashwagandha has been studied for many uses including arthritis, bipolar disorder, ADHD, insomnia, and others, however where it has proven most effective is in its ability to counteract stress. In a placebo-controlled study on 64 adults, those who took 300 mg twice daily of ashwagandha root extract for two months showed a 33 to 44 percent reduction in stress levels compared to baseline. In this same study, those who took the ashwagandha showed a 22 to 28 percent reduction in blood levels of cortisol, the body's stress hormone.[37] Similarly, two placebo-controlled trials have concluded that taking ashwagandha root is effective in decreasing anxiety compared to placebo.[38] [39] While more long-term research is needed, initial clinical studies appear positive in terms of ashwagandha's efficacy.

Is it safe?

Ashwagandha is considered safe and well tolerated when taken short term. It is best to limit continuous use of ashwagandha to 12 weeks. Avoid taking ashwagandha while pregnant or nursing. It has been associated with an increased risk for miscarriage. Ashwagandha may interact with certain drugs or conditions, so always speak with a healthcare provider before taking it. Specifically it can interact with diabetes and blood pressure medications, benzodiazepines (such as Xanax or Valium), sedatives, immunosuppressants, thyroid hormone, and herbs or supplements that are sedating or lower blood pressure. Similarly, it should be used with caution by those who have diabetes, high or low blood pressure, thyroid disease, autoimmune disease, or peptic ulcer disease. It should always be discontinued at least two weeks prior to surgery due to CNS depressant properties which may become dangerous when combined with anesthesia or other medications used during/after surgery.

BACOPA MONNIERI

Sustainability Score: 4/5 Stars

Bacopa monnieri is one of the oldest medicinal herbs known to man, with usage dating as far back as the beginning of Ayurvedic medicine.[40] As such, it's widely common in southeast Asian countries like India, Pakistan, Nepal, and Sri Lanka, but can be found growing in warm, damp environments around the world. Traditionally, it has been used to treat epilepsy, asthma, ulcers, tumors, and other maladies. Today, it is used as a nootropic to improve cognition and memory, while also reducing anxiety.

Does it work?

Preliminary studies have shown bacopa to be useful in improving cognitive function, however there has been variability between formulations. A 2001 placebo-controlled study using the KeenMind formulation of bacopa extract showed statistically significant improvements in information processing speed, learning rate, memory, and levels of anxiety after 12 weeks of use.[41] However, a 2002 placebo-controlled trial also using KeenMind showed improved retention of new information, but no benefit for attention, everyday memory, or anxiety levels.[42] An Australian study in 2010 demonstrated that a different formulation, BacoMind, improved memory acquisition and retention in elderly adults after 12 weeks of use[43]. Finally, a meta-analysis published in 2014, which included nine high-quality studies, showed that bacopa can enhance cognition and improve reaction time. However this benefit was only noted for the KeenMind formulation, not the others. These researchers concluded that bacopa may enhance cognition, but more research using a standardized formulation is still needed.[44] Bacopa does not appear to have short-term cognitive-enhancing effects when given in a single dose.[45]

Moreover, a study dated back to 1980 showed those who took bacopa experienced fewer symptoms of anxiety including nervousness, palpitations, insomnia, headache, and concentration problems.[46] And another study from 2014, using the BacoMind formulation, showed bacopa to be beneficial in decreasing symptoms of ADHD in children.[47]

Is it safe?

Bacopa is considered safe for short-term use (up to three months) in adults and children, however users commonly report side effects of stomach cramps, increased bowel movements, and nausea.

L-TYROSINE

Sustainability Score: 3/5 Stars

As an amino acid that helps build proteins, L-Tyrosine (or "tyrosine") can boost dopamine and adrenaline, influencing mood and sleep. Tyrosine is considered a "building block" of these chemicals, and it is therefore theorized that increasing the body's supply of it will result in greater production of them. While the science behind that theory is still yet to be proven, studies do suggest that increased tyrosine levels can reduce the brain and body's response to stress. As a nootropic, then, it is taken to help boost and maintain focus for a limited amount of time.

Does it work?

Most research has focused on the use of tyrosine for those with low levels of tyrosine in the blood due to a genetic condition called PKU. People with PKU are unable to process phenylalanine, an essential precursor to tyrosine, in the diet. For cognitive performance, the science on tyrosine is not as conclusive, but still promising. One study found participants performed better in memory and tracking tests, while also experiencing lower blood pressure.[48] A different study showed that acute tyrosine intake (two hours prior to cognitive testing) did not improve mood or reaction times.[49] Another study found that tyrosine helped reduce negative symptoms, "adverse moods," and performance deficiencies among participants exposed to extreme cold for more than four hours.[50] Yet another study found tyrosine dramatically boosted participants' wakefulness while maintaining their performance during a continuous period of overnight work.[51] It is important to note that all these studies were fairly limited in sample size, and more research with larger sample sizes is needed to validate these findings.

Is it safe?

Tyrosine is considered generally safe for use in moderate consumption over short-term periods (up to three months).[52] Because L-Tyrosine can affect neurotransmitter production and balance, we do not recommend consumption for more than three months.

PHOSPHATIDYLSERINE

Sustainability Score: 5/5 Stars

Phosphatidylserine, or PS for short, is one type of phospholipid naturally found in the body. Phospholipids are the fatty elements essential to the formation of cell membranes, and PS specifically is found abundantly in cell membranes of the brain. Since animal studies suggest that levels of PS in the brain decrease with age, it is thought that supplementing with PS can help preserve brain function and memory.[53] PS is also used to combat the symptoms of ADHD, especially inattention. In early research, scientists used PS from cattle brain cells. However, due to potential for viral transmission, PS supplements are now derived from plant sources (mostly soy).

Does it work?

Promising research suggests that PS is effective in improving memory and decreasing symptoms of ADHD. In elderly people showing early signs of cognitive decline, taking PS has been shown to be beneficial in supporting attention, verbal skills, and memory.[54][55] The benefits of taking PS can be enhanced when it is paired with omega-3 fatty acids. Two studies using a specific formulation of these two compounds demonstrated improvements in "immediate memory and sustained attention" compared to placebo in women who were complaining of memory problems.[56][57] Those who appeared to benefit the most were those with relatively good cognition to start.

Finally, preliminary research shows PS to be beneficial in lessening symptoms of ADHD. A 2014 placebo-controlled trial suggests that children ages 4-14 years who have never otherwise received treatment for ADHD showed improvements in inattention and hyperactivity scores after supplementing with PS for two months.[58]

Is it safe?

There are no known safety concerns with continuous use up to six months. Use extended beyond six months has not been studied. PS is also known to be safe in children ages 4-18 years in doses up to 300 mg per day. Users have experienced side effects including stomach upset, flatulence, insomnia, and headache.

CAFFEINE

Sustainability Score: 4/5 Stars

The world's most commonly consumed nootropic, caffeine, belongs to a group of compounds called methylxanthines and has several natural sources including coffee beans, cocoa beans, tea leaves, kola nuts, and guarana berries. Caffeine works by stimulating the autonomic nervous system and by blocking the action of a chemical in the body known as adenosine, which would otherwise cause drowsiness.[59] Thus it gets its popularity from its classic effects of enhancing the central nervous system, elevating heart rate and respiration, and for having mood-altering properties. Even athletes seek out caffeine to enhance performance. However, in high concentrations caffeine can be dangerous, even lethal, and in 2018 the FDA banned formulations sold in such high concentrations.

Does it work?

We all know from experience that caffeine does indeed work, but in case you were wondering about the research behind it, here it is. Where caffeine has proven most effective is in the treatment of headaches. Studies have consistently shown caffeine to be effective when used in conjunction with a pain reliever to treat headaches (both tension and migraine), and in the US it has reached FDA approval for this use.[60 61 62 63 64 65] The positive correlation between caffeine intake and staying alert throughout the day has also been well established.[66] [67] [68] [69] As little as 60 mg (amount typically in one cup of tea) can lead to a faster reaction time.[70] However, using caffeine to improve alertness and mental performance doesn't match up to getting a good night's sleep. One study from 2018 showed that coffee improved reaction times in those with or without poor sleep, however caffeine seemed to increase errors in the sleep deprived group. Additionally, this study showed that even with caffeine, the sleep deprived group did not score as well as those with adequate sleep, suggesting that caffeine does not fully compensate for inadequate sleep.[71] Some research suggests that taking caffeine along with l-theanine can improve cognitive performance better than either component alone.[72] [73] [74] [75] However, there is one study contradicting this correlation, and instead concluding l-theanine provides no added benefit to caffeine.[76] Regarding memory, caffeine intake between 65-200 mg daily may enhance memory in some individuals.[77] [78] However more research is needed to validate this conclusion.

Interestingly, there has been a positive correlation between caffeine intake in elderly women and a slowing of cognitive decline. One study showed that women ages 65-80 were 26 percent less likely to develop cognitive problems if they had more than 175 mg of caffeine per day.[79] And another study of 2,475 women over the age of 65 demonstrated that caffeine intake (particularly those who had > 371 mg/day) was associated with slower rates of cognitive decline. [80]

Is it safe?

Caffeine has been generally recognized as safe (GRAS) by the FDA. One cup of coffee contains roughly 80 to 175 mg of caffeine. Doses less than 400 mg per day typically do not result in adverse effects of elevated/irregular heart rate or sleep disturbance. It is recommended that pregnant women limit caffeine consumption to 200 mg/day. Toxic doses for an adult exceed 10 grams per day, much higher than typical consumption.

It is important to note that caffeine does have the potential to lead to what is called "drug dependence," a situation where after consistent use of a substance, abrupt discontinuation leads to withdrawal symptoms. In the case of caffeine withdrawal, symptoms include headache, irritability, and fatigue. One can also develop a "tolerance" to caffeine, meaning with chronic use of caffeine it may take a progressively higher dose to keep achieving the desired result.

RHODIOLA ROSEA

Sustainability Score: 4/5 Stars

As an adaptogen, the root of the rhodiola plant has been used in traditional medicine due to its proposed ability to help the body resist chemical and environmental stressors. Its use dates back to the first century AD, and today it is still commonly used for enhancing focus, stamina, and immunity, and decreasing anxiety, depression, and fatigue. Rhodiola rosea is named after the rose-like fragrance given off when the root is cut.

Does it work?

Despite its long-standing use in traditional medicine for a number of ailments, scientific evidence demonstrating its benefits is limited. There is some evidence to suggest it might enhance athletic performance in the short term. Two promising studies have shown that acute intake of rhodiola rosea extract is superior to placebo in augmenting endurance in young, healthy volunteers.[81] [82] However, taking rhodiola for four weeks does not seem to improve athleticism.[83] It may help to reduce muscle damage from some types of exercise, but marathon runners did not experience this benefit.[84] [85] Interestingly, results from one study looking at the effects of rhodiola on depression, another study looking at its effects on anxiety, and yet another looking at effects on life-stress have all shown rhodiola to be effective in these areas.[86] [87] [88] However more research is needed to support these conclusions. Finally, rhodiola does seem to be effective in combating fatigue. Studies on college students taking exams, night shift workers, and sleep deprived military cadets have shown taking rhodiola mitigates fatigue symptoms and may even improve mental clarity in these individuals.[89] [90] [91]

Is it safe?

Short-term use (up to ten weeks) of rhodiola is considered safe and well tolerated.

PANAX GINSENG

Sustainability Score: 3/5 Stars (avoid in pregnancy or while trying to conceive)

Another adaptogen, Panax ginseng is commonly used for improved cognition, athletic performance, energy, immunity, and stress reduction. It has many active components that affect various parts of the body, thus is considered beneficial for general wellness.

Does it work?

Promising evidence shows Panax ginseng improves "cognitive performance" in patients with Alzheimer's disease.[92] It has also been shown to be beneficial for cognition when taken by healthy young adults. One study showed 200 mg of Panax ginseng as one dose was superior to placebo in improving performances on certain cognitive tasks for up to six hours after the dose.[93] Regarding immunity, one interesting study found that those who took a particular formulation of Panax ginseng prior to and after receiving the influenza vaccination were 65 percent less likely to get the flu compared to placebo.[94] Some evidence suggests it can even fight fatigue in chronic fatigue sufferers.[95]

Is it safe?

Panax ginseng must be avoided in pregnancy. It has been shown to increase the risk of birth defects. Continuous use should also be limited to six months or less due to its hormone-like effects on the body.

GINKGO BILOBA

Sustainability Score: 3/5 (high doses are *toxic*; several disease and drug interactions but otherwise safe long term in appropriate doses)

By working as an antioxidant and by helping to increase blood flow in the body, ginkgo has been widely used for many medicinal purposes including dementia, anxiety, depression, vascular disease, glaucoma, heart disease, ADHD, autism, and even asthma. The ginkgo tree, also known as the maidenhair tree, is native to China and is one of the longest living species in the world, thought to have been in existence over 150 million years.

Does it work?

Ginkgo has been extensively cited in the medical literature for a myriad of health issues. Some of the important findings are highlighted here, but keep in mind this summation is not comprehensive. Regarding cognitive function in otherwise healthy adults, some small studies have demonstrated benefits. One study showed improvements in working memory after two days of ginkgo biloba extract at doses of 120 mg to 300 mg per day.[96] And there have been several studies with similar conclusions, although all of small sample size. Conversely, other small studies show no benefits on cognition in otherwise healthy adults.[97]

Moreover, ginkgo has been studied extensively when it comes to Alzheimer's and dementia. One large-scale review study concluded that taking ginkgo does seem to improve cognition in those with cognitive impairments, however results are "inconsistent and unpredictable."[98] A more recent randomized controlled trial from 2012 showed taking a specific ginkgo biloba extract (EGb 761) for 24 weeks at a dose of 240 mg daily improved cognition and functioning in patients with either Alzheimer's disease or vascular dementia.[99] However, ginkgo has not been shown to be superior to prescription drugs for the treatment of dementia.[100] [101] In regards to prevention, ginkgo has not been shown to be effective in preventing Alzheimer's disease or dementia.[102] [103]

Ginkgo has been shown to be effective in reducing symptoms of anxiety. A 2007 publication in the *Journal of Psychiatric Research* showed that those who took a specific ginkgo biloba extract (EGb 761) experienced a greater reduction in anxiety symptoms than those who took placebo. Those who took the higher dose of EGb 761 (480 mg daily) experienced a greater reduction in symptoms after four weeks of treatment than those who took the lower dose (240 mg daily).[104]

Ginkgo biloba's benefit for those with peripheral vascular disease is also an area of research interest with conflicting results. A randomized, double-blind clinical trial showed taking the specific extract EGb 761 for 24 weeks decreased pain symptoms while walking for those with vascular disease. Those who took 240 mg daily experienced a greater reduction in symptoms than those who took 120 mg daily.[105] However a similar study showed no improvements after a shorter duration of treatment (16 weeks).[106]

Is it safe?

Available research shows gingko leaf extract can be taken safely in appropriate doses long term. Higher doses at or above 100-2000 mg/kg five times per week for two years has shown to be unsafe in animal models and can even be cancer-causing.[107] However this is a much higher dose than the typical human dose of 100-300 mg per day. Others have reported severe allergic reactions from consuming fresh ginkgo. It can thin the blood, so it should always be discontinued at least two weeks prior to surgery.

Always check with your doctor before taking ginkgo as it can interfere with some conditions and medications. Ginkgo supplements should be avoided in those who are pregnant or nursing as they have hormone-like effects that may lead to preterm labor. It should also be avoided in those who have bleeding or clotting disorders or those who take medications to prevent blood clotting.

Avoid taking ginkgo if you also take ibuprofen, warfarin (Coumadin), or any other medications used to slow blood clotting; alprazolam (Xanax), buspirone (BuSpar), efavirenz (Sustiva), fluoxetine (Prozac), or trazodone (Desyrel). Those who take medications for anxiety, diabetes, or seizures should be especially cautious. Always check with your doctor before taking ginkgo if you take any medications metabolized by the liver (especially those metabolized by the following enzymes: CYP1A2, CYP2C19, CYP2C9, CYP2D6, and CYP3A4), or if you take medications that lower seizure threshold.

One should always avoid consuming fresh ginkgo leaves or seeds as these can be toxic and have been shown to cause breathing difficulty, seizures, loss of consciousness, and even death.[108]

CHAPTER THREE

UNSUSTAINABLE NOOTROPICS

NICOTINE

Sustainability Score: 2/5 Stars (for highly addictive properties and severe discontinuation symptoms)

One of the most highly sought-after drugs, nicotine has been used for decades for that quick high, and its stimulant effects are highly addictive. Aside from leading to dependence, nicotine itself is not thought to present health hazards when used in normal doses for otherwise healthy, non-pregnant adults. It is the tobacco in cigarettes and other nicotine products which puts users at risk for many types of cancer and other negative health consequences.[1] And with nicotine's high potential for abuse and dependence, many nicotine-only products (e.g., nicotine patches) are used to help users quit using tobacco products as well as to minimize withdrawal symptoms during the quitting process. However, the potential health risks of using nicotine-only products, particularly e-cigarettes, remain controversial.[2]

Does it work?

Nicotine is known for its widespread recreational use because it is highly effective in producing quick brain stimulation and elevations in mood.[3] However, nicotine leads to dependence within just days of use.[4] Medicinally, nicotine products such as patches, lozenges, and gum deliver a lower dose of nicotine allowing the user to slowly stop using nicotine, ideally without withdrawal symptoms. These methods are reported to increase the rate of quitting by 50 to 70 percent.[5]

Is it safe?

Nicotine is quick to lead to addiction and dependence. Withdrawal symptoms from nicotine include depressed mood and irritability, anxiety, trouble sleeping, concentration problems, restlessness, slowing of heart rate, and increased appetite.[6] Nicotine should be avoided by youth and adolescents, by those who are pregnant, and by those with heart conditions.[7][8] Additionally, nicotine can lead to toxicity and can be lethal in high doses.[9][10] Those who employ nicotine-only products to help with smoking cessation report headache, mouth irritation (inhaler only), acne, gum disease, nausea, diarrhea, back pain, joint pain, sinusitis, and other adverse effects.

5-HTP

Sustainability Score: 1/5 Stars

5-HTP (5-Hydroxytryptophan) is a chemical byproduct of L-tryptophan, one of the body's essential amino acids. It is often used to combat disorders such as insomnia, depression, anxiety, severe headaches and migraines, fibromyalgia, attention deficit hyperactivity disorder, seizures, and Parkinson's disease. It is also sometimes used to treat symptoms and disorders related to menstruation. It works by increasing the serotonin levels in the brain, which affects sleep, mood, appetite, memory, learning, and sexual function. Users taking it as a nootropic believe it can help optimize the brain by balancing serotonin and dopamine levels. It is sold over the counter as an herbal supplement and is not FDA approved.

Does it work?

While no conclusive studies have been performed, available evidence from several smaller studies suggest that 5-HTP is superior to placebo in alleviating symptoms of depression. The challenge here is that not all these studies have been conducted with full scientific rigor, and thus the findings are anecdotal and not as reliable.[11]

Other studies have found positive impacts on patients with fibromyalgia and migraines.[12][13] Additionally, some studies have findings that suggest 5-HTP may be a good weight loss aid by acting as an appetite suppressant.[14]

Is it safe?

5-HTP is generally considered safe, but it has been linked to eosinophilia-myalgia syndrome (EMS) in "rare cases." Symptoms of EMS include "extreme muscle tenderness" and blood abnormalities.[15] Additionally, taking too much 5-HTP can result in serotonin spikes, which can lead to nervousness, anxiety, and negative feelings of self-worth. Severe serotonin overload can also lead to "serotonin syndrome," with symptoms including high fever, irregular heartbeat, seizures, and unconsciousness.[16] For this reason, those who are taking prescribed antidepressants should generally avoid 5-HTP. Lastly, because 5-HTP makes you sleepy, it's advised to not combine 5-HTP with any chemicals that also cause sleepiness, as well as to avoid driving or operating machinery.

AMPHETAMINE / DEXTROAMPHETAMINE

Sustainability Score: 1/5 Stars

Known commercially as Adderall, this drug is available by prescription only and is reserved for those struggling with concentration and hyperactivity due to ADHD (attention deficit hyperactivity disorder). Amphetamines work by increasing the release of catecholamines (dopamine and norepinephrine)

in the brain, essentially enabling the user to remain calm and focused. And while extremely effective for both children and adults in treating symptoms of ADHD, users often struggle with long-term use of amphetamines due to unwanted side effects, primarily appetite suppression and insomnia.

Does it work?

Certainly, the science behind these stimulants show that they are effective at treating ADHD, but studies have also shown that they are effective at enhancing cognition at "low, clinically relevant doses."[17] A separate analysis of 48 studies found these stimulants to also enhance a user's ability to control their inhibitions and speed up short-term memory formation.[18]

Is it safe?

Like similar stimulants, it's important for users to understand that this category of drug has a high potential for abuse and dependence, and abrupt discontinuation can lead to depression, extreme fatigue, nausea, and other symptoms.[19] Common side effects from taking amphetamines include weight loss, insomnia, agitation, dry mouth, stomach cramps, headache, diarrhea, fever, nervousness, and others. What's more, stimulants can dramatically raise your heart rate and blood pressure. Those with preexisting heart problems are at risk for serious cardiovascular events including sudden death, stroke, or heart attack. Moreover these drugs should be used with caution with other drugs that increase levels of serotonin, including many antidepressants, due to risk for serotonin syndrome. [20]

ANIRACETAM

Sustainability Score: 1/5 Stars

Presumed to be more potent than piracetam, aniracetam belongs to the racetam class of drugs, and is thought to work by interacting with a specific glutamate receptor in the brain called AMPA. Aniracetam is a drug available by prescription in Europe, but does not carry FDA approval in the US. It is being investigated for its use among patients with dementia as well as those prone to developing similar brain disorders. As a nootropic, it is generally used to combat anxiety and depression.

Does it work?

One large analysis showed positive effects of aniracetam in reducing the symptoms of vascular dementia, particularly in younger patients.[21] A single small study found that even in healthy patients, aniracetam improved cognitive performance and functionality, while also improving patients' emotional state.[22]

Is it safe?

Aniracetam is not FDA approved, and while there is a lot of anecdotal evidence to both its efficacy and safety, there appears to be little clinical evidence either way. That said, users of the compound have reported increased anxiety and heart rate, lack of appetite, nausea, fatigue, and other potentially harmful side effects.[23]

LEVOCARNITINE

Sustainability Score: 2/5 Stars

Levocarnitine (or L-carnitine) is an amino acid found naturally in the body that plays an essential role in energy production by transporting fatty acids within mitochondrial cells. Natural dietary sources of L-carnitine include dairy products and meat. The body can also make its own L-carnitine by a process in the liver and kidneys. Most of the body's L-carnitine is harbored in muscles, and to a much lesser extent it is found in the bloodstream. While the body is able to convert L-carnitine to other forms of carnitine (such as acetyl carnitine and propionyl carnitine), it is unclear whether medicinal benefits of the various forms are interchangeable, thus it is important to note this particular monograph pertains to L-carnitine or Levocarnitine specifically.

As a supplement, L-carnitine is often used by healthcare providers to treat L-carnitine deficiency due to a rare genetic condition called "inborn errors of metabolism." It is also helpful for patients who experience carnitine deficiency secondary to hemodialysis or drugs which may lower levels of carnitine and is a treatment option for those who experience toxicity from a common seizure medication known as valproate or valproic acid (brand name Depakote). It can be used to counteract myopathies due to zidovudine (a medication for

HIV/AIDs) or isotretinoin (a medication for acne). Several other uses include, but are not limited to: heart disease, anorexia and undesirable weight loss, chronic fatigue syndrome, diabetes, celiac disease, male fertility, memory and athletic enhancement, and autism and ADHD.

Does it work?

Levocarnitine has been studied extensively, and found to be effective for its primary medicinal purposes of treating carnitine deficiency from very specific causes, such as medication toxicity or inborn errors of metabolism.[24] [25] When taken for athletic performance, results are conflicting. Some studies show that taking L-carnitine enhances athletic performance,[26] [27] while others do not.[28] [29] Carnitine has not been shown to be effective when taken for fatigue or cognitive improvements.[30] [31] While carnitine supplementation does appear to benefit behaviors in those with autism,[32] it has not shown to be effective for ADHD.[33]

Is it safe?

Humans with healthy liver and kidney functions

and who eat dietary sources of carnitine generally do not need to take L-carnitine supplements, and doses of L-carnitine beyond three grams/day can result in "nausea, vomiting, abdominal cramps, and 'fishy' body odor." There appears to also be a risk that carnitine can be metabolized to TMAO that "might increase the risk of cardiovascular disease."[34]

CREATINE

Sustainability Score: 2/5 Stars

Similar to carnitine, creatine plays an important role in metabolizing food into energy. It is naturally found in red meat and seafood, but the body also produces it naturally. It is known for improving athletic performance, and is one of the most prevalent compounds in athletic supplements. It is also being investigated for its ability to boost cognitive functions.

Does it work?

Studies suggest that creatine is highly effective for improving athletic performance, particularly for activities involving short, high-intensity activities. It appears that increasing the "creatine pool" in the body helps in muscle formation at the cellular level, improves muscular recovery times between training periods, and generally improves workout quality and enhanced performance. Other studies looking at the neurological effects of increasing creatine in the body have suggested improved brain functions, specifically in older patients facing cognitive decline.[35]

Is it safe?

Most studies have examined the short-term effects of creatine supplements, but fewer studies have looked at any long-term effects. Reported side effects include increased risk of kidney disease or even failure, increased water retention, nausea, diarrhea, cramping and muscle pain, and high blood pressure. It is recommended that people with liver or kidney disease should avoid taking additional creatine.[36]

DONEPEZIL

Sustainability Score: 2/5 Stars

Donepezil (trade name Aricept) is an FDA-approved prescription medication for the treatment of dementia and Alzheimer's disease. Given its cognitive boosting properties, it has also been observed for its effects on otherwise healthy individuals.

Does it work?

There has been a lot of media buzz in recent years about the cognitive-enhancement powers of donepezil, though one study found that to be more hype than fact.[37] That said, a literature review found reported improved cognitive performance.[38] And a more comprehensive study found that donepezil improved cognitive function in Alzheimer's patients, though researchers are hesitant to make predictions about outcomes or long-term effects.[39]

Is it safe?

Donepezil is FDA approved for treating Alzheimer's patients at all stages.[40] Reported side effects include nausea, vomiting, diarrhea, loss of appetite, dizziness, drowsiness, weakness, and others.[41]

HUPERZINE A

Sustainability Score: N/A (more research is needed)

A component of the Chinese medicinal herb, Chinese club moss, Huperzine A is another compound used for fighting Alzheimer's disease and other dementias as well as a muscle disease called myasthenia gravis. It is also employed by healthy individuals to enhance cognitive abilities and athletic performance. It works by increasing acetylcholine levels in the brain.

Does it work?

A 2013 meta-analysis of 20 randomized clinical trials concluded that Huperzine A seems to be effective in improving "cognitive function, daily living activity, and global clinical assessment" in patients suffering from Alzheimer's disease.[42] It may also enhance memory in healthy individuals and help combat cognitive decline in those with mild cognitive impairment.[43] [44] However more research, including placebo-controlled and randomized-controlled trials, is needed.

Is it safe?

Generally considered safe with short-term use, Huperzine A may carry the following side effects: "nausea, diarrhea, vomiting, sweating, blurred vision, slurred speech," and others.[45] It is important to note, Huperzine A is also known as selagine, not to be confused with our next compound, selegiline. This herb extract could be a sustainably safe and effective compound, but we found the long-term research on safety severely lacking for us to give Huperzine A a score.

SELEGILINE (ELDEPRYL)

Sustainability Score: 2/5 Stars

Selegiline falls under a class of medications known as monoamine oxidase inhibitors (MAO-Is for short), used to treat depression as well as symptoms of Parkinson's disease. It works by increasing the amount of dopamine in the brain. It is unique in the fact that it was the first drug created to selectively inhibit monoamine oxidase type B, thus it is technically an MAO Type B Inhibitor. It has been FDA approved for Parkinson's disease and for major depressive disorder when used as a transdermal patch (brand name Emsam) but is also sometimes used off label for ADHD.

Does it work?

Selegiline is often employed as an adjunct agent to levodopa/carbidopa therapy for patients with Parkinson's disease to allow patients to take a lower dose of the levodopa/carbidopa, which can be associated with abnormal movements and other motor complications.[46] There is controversial evidence that it may even slow the progression of Parkinson's disease.[47] As a transdermal patch, selegiline also provides relief for those suffering from major depressive disorder.[48]

Is it safe?

When taken in pill form, the most prominent risks associated with the use of selegiline are extremely high blood pressure, allergic reaction, and serotonin syndrome. The transdermal patch carries a Black Box Warning for increased suicidal thoughts and behaviors.

METHYLPHENIDATE

Sustainability Score: 1/5 Stars

Another prescription stimulant for the treatment of ADHD, methylphenidate is sold under several brand names including Ritalin, Aptensio, Concerta, Metadate, Quillivant, Methylin, and others. Adderall is called "prescription grade amphetamines," and methylphenidate is called "prescription grade cocaine."

It is highly effective in improving attention and controlling hyperactive behaviors, but like amphetamines, comes with a host of side effects and potential risks when used long-term or inappropriately.

Does it work?

Methylphenidate has been widely used to treat ADHD.[49] You may also see it prescribed for narcolepsy and binge-eating disorders.[50] In more recent years, various forms of methylphenidate have become prominent in the drug market for its stimulant effects. Researchers consider this an "uprising threat" and encourage greater widespread education regarding risks associated with methylphenidate to avoid imminent "intoxications and fatalities" in the years to come." [51]

Is it safe?

Methylphenidate is an FDA-approved drug for treating ADHD and is one of the most prescribed drugs in the United States.[52] That said, it is not without side effects, which include nervousness, loss of appetite, weight loss, dizziness, nausea, vomiting, and others. Like amphetamines, those with preexisting structural heart conditions are at risk for sudden death, stroke, and heart attack. It also carries the risk of hypersensitivity reactions, peripheral vascular complications, and priapism (prolonged painful or non-painful erections sometimes requiring surgical intervention).

MODAFINIL

Sustainability Score: 2/5 Stars

Sold under the commercial name Provigil, modafinil is an FDA-approved medication for treating daytime sleepiness disorders such as narcolepsy or obstructive sleep apnea. It is also used off-label for ADHD, cancer-related fatigue, depression, and fatigue related to multiple sclerosis. Some even believe modafinil to have cognitive-enhancing properties. The exact way modafinil works is unknown, but it has been shown to increase dopamine levels in the brain.

Does it work?

Research fully supports the effects of modafinil for those with disorders associated with sleep deprivation.[53] However, evidence regarding its use for cognitive enhancement is inconclusive.[54]

Is it safe?

Common side effects often include headaches, anxiety, difficulty with falling asleep, and nausea. Some users have experienced anaphylactic allergic reactions, skin reactions including life-threatening Stevens-Johnson syndrome, and even hallucinations. It is not recommended for those with kidney or liver issues, heart disease, or seizures.

PHENIBUT

Sustainability Score: 1/5 Stars (for highly addictive properties and severe discontinuation symptoms)

Phenibut is a central nervous system depressant that acts similarly to the prescription muscle relaxant, baclofen.[55] It is thought to have cognitive-enhancing properties, however research is lacking to support this theory. It is mostly used to treat anxiety, fear, insomnia, stress, fatigue, post-traumatic stress disorder (PTSD), and depression, among others. It is widely used in Russia, but is less prevalent in other parts of the world. It is also known to be used recreationally due to its euphoric effects and can lead to addiction and withdrawal.

Does it work?

The science behind phenibut is lacking. One Russian study has shown it to be effective in the treatment of chronic fatigue, particularly among patients with poor blood circulation in their brain.[56] Other studies have been conducted to examine phenibut's impact on ADHD, anxiety, cognition, headaches, neuroprotection, and other topics.[57]

While it is available commercially in the US, it is not FDA approved.

Is it safe?

Case reports and case series have reported adverse effects including nausea, dizziness, poor balance, fatigue, and feelings of electric shocks in the arms and legs.[58] Phenibut is a psychoactive drug that can lead to severe dependency and withdrawal symptoms such as anxiety, agitation, and hallucinations. Moreover, high doses of phenibut can lead to toxicity.

PIRACETAM

Sustainability Score: 2/5 Stars (for lack of sufficient research on long-term safety and lack of FDA approval)

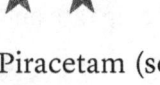

Piracetam (sold under many brand names) is a medication approved as a prescription treatment for myoclonus (involuntary muscle twitching), but does not carry FDA approval in the US. Commercially it is branded as a powerful nootropic with purported cognitive-enhancing properties. It is presumed to work by increasing blood flow to the brain. Piracetam is particularly noteworthy because it is "extremely well tolerated" and little to no adverse effects have been reported.[59] [60]

Does it work?

Despite much research, the science on piracetam is inconclusive. Several large-scale scientific reviews have examined the effects of piracetam on dementia with conflicting results. A 2001 review concluded evidence is lacking to support this indication while a 2002 and 2005 review identified a true benefit for elderly patients with dementia.[61] [62] [63]

Is it safe?

Available clinical evidence suggests piracetam is very well tolerated with side effects being rare and transient. These can include anxiety, insomnia, headache, agitation, somnolence, weight gain, and others.

ADAPTOGENS &
MUSHROOMS

CHAPTER FOUR

ADAPTOGENS, MUSHROOMS, AND ANTI-INFLAMMATORIES

Human beings have evolved in large part due to our advanced nervous system, which takes stimuli from our environment and translates them into sensations. Our bodies in turn react to these sensations by producing chemicals in our brain that help us cope with the environment.

Although this system has helped shape us over the hundreds of thousands of years of human evolution, today's modern world offers a number of environmental stimuli that simply didn't exist in the past. Think smartphones, traffic, pollution, etc.

Enter the world of adaptogens. The concept is simple: use naturally occurring compounds that humans have relied on for thousands of years to help regulate the nervous system.

And this is one of the most interesting things about nootropics: they don't have to be chemical compounds, at least not in the modern medical sense. Some of them are synthesized based on what scientists know about the chemicals and their sources. But some of them are naturally found in a variety of foods and plants as well, and can be extracted from those sources.

Let's take a look at some of the more well-known and popular ones, along with some other supplements that are naturally occurring and even vital to the human body. In our attempt to be as scientifically-driven as possible, generally speaking, the research on adaptogens is growing but very scarce, and therefore, many compounds in this chapter do not have sufficient research for us to give them a sustainability score.

ADAPTOGENS

AMLA

Sustainability Score: N/A (more research needed)

Also known as the *Indian Gooseberry*, amla has a long history of use in Ayurvedic medicine, and the tree is in fact considered sacred by Hindus. From the roots to the fruits, all parts of the plant are used in traditional herbal preparations. Based on its cultural associations, amla is believed to help bolster the immune system, reduce inflammation, and improve energy. Traditional scientific research has generally overlooked amla, but it has been shown to work in reducing cholesterol levels in those with high cholesterol or normal cholesterol levels at baseline.[1]

ELEUTHERO

Sustainability Score: N/A (more research needed)

Also known as "Siberian Ginseng," eleuthero has origins in traditional medicine, with its roots, leaves, and berries being used across East Asia, China, Japan, and Russia. It has traditionally been used to promote cardiovascular health, improve mood, and boost energy. Clinical research has shown that taking a specific formulation that includes both siberian ginseng and andrographis can help speed recovery from the common cold.[2] It also may work to improve athletic performance[3] and cognitive performance,[4] but more research is still needed to verify these findings. Siberian ginseng does not seem to be effective in reducing stress.[5]

HOLY BASIL

Sustainability Score: N/A (more research needed, do not take while pregnant or trying to conceive)

This is not your garden-variety basil. Holy Basil is a plant native to India and is even considered sacred by the Hindus. It has been used in Ayurvedic medicine to combat stress and anxiety and is also used in Hindu religious ceremonies. Additionally, it is a common ingredient for cooking Thai dishes and in this setting is referred to as "hot basil." Though not much scientific research has been conducted on holy basil's effects, it has been tested for its antioxidant properties.[6] It has also been shown to be effective in lowering anxiety and anxiety-related depression when taken in a dose of 500 mg twice daily after meals for 60 days.[7] Avoid taking Holy Basil when pregnant or trying to conceive. It has been shown to decrease implantation rate when taken in high doses.[8] It can also decrease male fertility.[9]

MACA

Sustainability Score: N/A (more research needed)

A root native to Peru, maca is known as "Peruvian ginseng," and is a staple of indigenous people of the Andes. It has been used to address anemia, fatigue, sexual dysfunction related to antidepressants, fertility, and libido. The available medical literature suggests taking maca may enhance semen quality among young healthy men, however more research is still needed.[10] Moreover, taking maca may attenuate sexual dysfunction that may occur as a side effect of SSRI antidepressant use in postmenopausal women.[11] However, other reviews and studies have not found significant evidence of maca's effect on men's sexual function.[12]

RHODIOLA ROSEA (REPRODUCED HERE FROM THE "NOOTROPICS" SECTION)

Sustainability Score: N/A (more research is needed)

As an adaptogen, the root of the rhodiola plant has been used in traditional medicine due to its proposed ability to help the body resist chemical and environmental stressors. Its use dates back to the first century AD, and today it is still commonly used for enhancing focus, stamina, and immunity, and decreasing anxiety, depression, and fatigue. Rhodiola rosea is named after the rose-like fragrance given off when the root is cut.

Despite its long-standing use in traditional medicine for a number of ailments, scientific evidence demonstrating its benefits is limited. There is some evidence to suggest it might enhance athletic performance in the short term. Two promising studies have shown that acute intake of rhodiola rosea extract is superior to placebo in augmenting endurance in young, healthy volunteers.[13] [14] However, taking rhodiola for four weeks does not seem to improve athleticism.[15] It may help to reduce muscle damage from some types of exercise, but marathon runners were not shown to experience this benefit.[16] [17] Interestingly, results from one study looking at the effects of rhodiola on depression, another study looking at its effects on anxiety, and yet another looking at effects on life-stress have all shown rhodiola to be effective in these areas.[18] [19] [20] However more research is needed to support these conclusions. Finally, rhodiola does seem to be effective in combating fatigue. Studies on college students taking exams, night shift workers, and sleep deprived military cadets have shown taking rhodiola mitigates fatigue symptoms and may even improve mental clarity in these individuals.[21] [22] [23]

Short-term use (up to 10 weeks) of rhodiola is considered safe and well tolerated.

ASHWAGANDHA (REPRODUCED HERE FROM THE "NOOTROPICS" SECTION)

Sustainability Score: 4/5 Stars (not to be taken while pregnant)

Ashwagandha is a plant and its roots and berries are used for medicinal purposes. Primarily it is used as an "adaptogen," meaning it is intended to reduce stress levels in the body.

Ashwagandha has been studied for many uses including arthritis, bipolar disorder, ADHD, insomnia and others, however where it has proven most effective is in its ability to counteract stress. In a placebo-controlled study on 64 adults, those who took 300 mg twice daily of ashwagandha root extract for 2 months showed a 33 to 44 percent reduction in stress levels compared to baseline. In this same study, those who took the ashwagandha showed a 22 to 28 percent reduction in blood levels of cortisol, the body's stress hormone.[24] Similarly, two placebo-controlled trials have concluded that taking ashwagandha root is effective in decreasing anxiety compared to placebo.[25] [26] While more long-term research is needed, initial clinical studies appear positive in terms of ashwagandha's efficacy.

Ashwagandha is considered safe and well tolerated when taken short term. It is best to limit continuous use of ashwagandha to 12 weeks. Avoid taking ashwagandha while pregnant or nursing. It has been associated with an increased risk for miscarriage. Ashwagandha may interact with certain drugs or conditions, so always speak with a healthcare provider before taking it. Specifically it can interact with diabetes and blood pressure medications, benzodiazepines (such as Xanax or Valium), sedatives, immunosuppressants, thyroid hormone, and herbs or supplements that are sedating or lower blood pressure. Similarly, it should be used with caution by those who have diabetes, high or low blood pressure, thyroid disease, autoimmune disease, or peptic ulcer disease. It should always be discontinued at least two weeks prior to surgery due to CNS depressant properties, which may become dangerous when combined with anesthesia or other medications used during/after surgery.

MUSHROOMS

Mushrooms can flexibly qualify as an adaptogen ("stress relieving agent") and some, like Lion's Mane, can also qualify as a cognitive-enhancing agent within the "nootropic" category.

LION'S MANE

Sustainability Score: 5/5 Stars

This flowing fungus, also known as "monkey head mushroom," has a long history of both medicinal and culinary uses across Asia, Europe, and North America. Lion's mane mushroom is thought to have many medicinal and neuroprotective properties, and while human studies are scarce, animal studies have shown promising effects including lowering cholesterol levels, combating stomach ulcers, lower blood sugar and decreasing neuropathic pain from diabetes, and synthesizing NGF (nerve growth factor) which may suggest a therapeutic role in neurodegenerative brain disorders.[27] [28] [29] [30] [31] An interesting study on mice in 2017 evaluated a specific Lion's mane protein called HEP3 and its potential for enhancing immune function by working through the gut.[32] In human studies, Lion's mane extract has shown to be better than placebo in improving mild cognitive impairment and in reducing symptoms of depression and anxiety. [33] [34]

CHAGA

Sustainability Score: N/A (more research needed)

Typically found growing on birch trees, traditional medicines in Russia and Asia have used chaga mushroom to boost the immune system. Typically, the mushroom is ground into a fine powder and then brewed as a tea or even fermented. Traditional health claims have been somewhat substantiated by science, finding that the fungus has significant antioxidant properties, which can help reduce inflammation but also slow or fight cancer growth.[35] [36]Additionally, the mushroom is high in fiber, which likely helps contribute to initial findings of its ability to help lower bad cholesterol and increase good cholesterol.[37] Unfortunately, human studies observing the effects of this mushroom are lacking, thus conclusions cannot be drawn regarding its benefits or safety.

MAITAKE

Sustainability Score: 5/5 Stars

Another mushroom that is traditionally found in Japan and China, maitake is also known as "Hen of the Woods." Traditionally, it's been used to treat diabetes and hypertension, but in modern medicine the testing of this fungus to prevent and treat cancer is quite promising. One preclinical study, for example, found compounds in maitake helped to shrink tumors and reduce the number of cells that suppress the immune system.[38] Another in vitro study found that maitake can actually destroy breast cancer cells and suppress the formation of tumors in the breast.[39] And finally, a small study on humans showed an increase in a specific type of immune cell, called the NK cell, in cancer patients.[40] Much more research is needed, but maitake does appear to have powerful medicinal properties. It is important to note that maitake should be avoided in those who are pregnant/nursing or those with an autoimmune condition or bleeding disorder. It should also be used with caution in those with diabetes or high blood pressure and should be discontinued two weeks prior to any surgery.

CORDYCEPS

Sustainability Score: N/A (more research needed)

Cordyceps is a parasitic fungus that lives on caterpillars most commonly found in warm, humid climates, particularly in Southeast Asia. While scientific research is limited, cordyceps supplements are widely used for liver or kidney problems, male sexual problems, athletic performance, or for enhancing the immune system. In at least one preliminary study, cordyceps were found to help reduce the spread of cancerous cells.[41]

ANTI-INFLAMMATORIES

Inflammation occurs as a symptom in the body for a number of widespread health issues, including cardiovascular diseases and cancer, among others. It is the body's natural response to injury, and is commonly understood as a way of sending a signal to the immune system to heal or repair damaged tissues. In other words, the same thing that happens when you stub your toe also happens when you have internal health issues.

Luckily, nature has provided us with a number of items that traditional medicines have used to great effect. Following are three key anti-inflammatories you can easily find at your local grocery store!

TURMERIC CURCUMIN

Sustainability Score: 5/5 Stars

Traditional medicine's use of turmeric goes back millennia. Curcumin is its most active component and composes roughly 5 percent of raw turmeric. When used for cooking, it's the curcumin which gives foods such as curry its yellow color. However, turmeric curcumin alone has a low bioavailability, thus is best absorbed when combined with black pepper. You may also find that some formulations use bromelain to help with absorption. Turmeric curcumin has a long-standing use as an anti-inflammatory, antihyperlipidemic, antioxidant, antimicrobial, and immunostimulant. And many of these uses are supported by research. Preclinical animal trials have demonstrated its antioxidant, anti-inflammatory, antimicrobial, and even cancer-fighting properties.[42] [43] Clinically, medical providers often recommend turmeric to arthritis patients to help decrease inflammation and thus pain. Preliminary studies show it to be effective for this use.[44] It is also thought to be very effective in relieving stomach ulcers.[45] And one very promising placebo-controlled trial showed curcumin to be equally effective as Prozac in decreasing symptoms of depression.[46]

As with all supplements, appropriate dosage is important and very high doses of turmeric curcumin must be avoided as this can cause heart arrhythmia. It must also be taken with caution in those who have bleeding disorders, iron deficiency, or diabetes and should be avoided altogether by those who have gallstones or other gallbladder problems. Those who are pregnant or nursing should avoid medicinal amounts of turmeric, but it is considered safe to consume amounts commonly found in food. There is a potential for turmeric to decrease male fertility.

GINGER

Sustainability Score: 5/5 Stars

Ginger and turmeric are actually closely related, and ginger also has a very long history of use in traditional medicine to fight nausea and help with digestion. In addition to generally helping with digestion, ginger can help stop or prevent vomiting, important for both pregnant women facing morning sickness and cancer patients reacting to chemotherapy.[47][48] It has also been tested as an analgesic and anti-inflammatory to offset pain associated with rigorous exercise.[49] It has even been studied for its properties to lower blood sugar levels in patients with type 2 diabetes.[50]

Ginger is typically well tolerated when taken in

normal doses, however when taken in higher doses, such as five grams daily, side effects of abdominal discomfort or heartburn may be more likely.

SPIRULINA

Sustainability Score: 5/5 Stars

Unlike turmeric and ginger, spirulina is not a spice but a consumable algae, and falls under the family of "blue-green algae." Spirulina is thought to be rich in B-vitamins, protein, and iron and has been employed for a variety of conditions including high cholesterol, high blood pressure, diabetes, ADHD, PMS, stress, depression, anxiety, and more. Specifically, studies have shown promising results when spirulina is used to lower cholesterol and reduce blood pressure. [51] [52]It has even been found to help improve athletic performance by increasing endurance.[53]

Spirulina is considered generally safe when known to be non-contaminated. However, contamination with toxic microcystins and heavy metals is possible, thus one must always remain cautious when consuming these supplements; spirulina should always be avoided in infants and children, and those who are pregnant or nursing.

CHAPTER FIVE

MORE ON COFFEE AND COFFEE ALTERNATIVES

COFFEE

Sustainability Score: 4/5 Stars

Coffee, one of those most popular approaches to caffeine consumption worldwide, is for many people a nonnegotiable start to the day. And while some are content after a single cup to jumpstart mental alertness, others rely on several cups daily to maintain their desired level of functioning. Coffee comes from brewed coffee beans, which are actually dried seeds from berries in the Caffea species. While native to Ethiopia and Sudan, coffee is now part of the agriculture of 70 countries with Brazil currently being the top producer.

Does it work?

Cognitive effects. Research shows that while coffee in moderation does in fact improve mood and concentration, higher doses may actually adversely affect productivity. One study from 1997 demonstrated that a 250 mg dose of caffeine produced favorable effects of enhanced mood and cognitive performance, however those who received a 500 mg dose of caffeine experienced "performance disruption" as well as unpleasant side effects including anxiety, irritability, nausea, and palpitations.[1]

Cardiovascular effects. Coffee's effects on the heart are controversial, but most medical providers recommend those with heart conditions to limit consumption. We know that excess consumption can lead to rapid or irregular heartbeat in the short term.[2] Yet, some studies suggest coffee does not increase one's risk for developing heart conditions, such as atrial fibrillation, even when consumed in amounts exceeding five cups per day.[3] [4] However, once a heart condition has been diagnosed, coffee (and any form of caffeine) should be consumed in moderation because of the proven effects of rapid and irregular heartbeats caused by caffeine. [5]

Hormonal effects. We know that caffeine increases the body's production of cortisol and that chronic daily caffeine consumption may reduce the body's amount of cortisol it produces in response, due to habituation to the caffeine. But it is unknown how coffee specifically affects cortisol production and how long that extra cortisol lingers in the body once it is triggered by caffeine.[6]

Established benefits. While research has been abundant and controversial, some benefits of coffee have been largely established. It has been long known that consuming 150 mg of caffeine has been proven to enhance cognitive performance for 10 hours or more.[7] And recent research has actually suggested that moderate consumption of coffee specifically (again 400 mg daily or less) is associated with a reduced risk for developing type 2 diabetes, Alzheimer's disease, and some types of cancer.[8] [9] Caffeine also causes vasoconstriction by binding to adenosine receptors in the brain, thus is commonly used for the treatment of migraine or post lumbar puncture headache. [10]

Is it safe?

On average, a single 8 oz cup of brewed coffee contains about 80 mg of caffeine. While moderate coffee consumption (up to five cups daily, or 400 mg of caffeine) is considered safe and well tolerated by the FDA, consuming coffee in excess amounts may have ramifications.[11] It is important to keep in mind that caffeine amounts vary depending on how the coffee is prepared, and also that each individual's sensitivity to caffeine can vary greatly depending on genetics, preexisting conditions, pregnancy, and taking certain medications. Known side effects of excess caffeine consumption include sleeping problems, anxious or depressed mood, rapid heart rate, nausea or heartburn, headache, and shakiness. Many of these same side effects can be seen in those who experience abrupt discontinuation, aka caffeine withdrawal. In extreme cases, when caffeine is consumed quickly and in large amounts (1g-1.5g), toxic effects can be observed.[12] [13]

BLACK AND GREEN TEA

Sustainability Score: 5/5 Stars

Both black and green tea come from the same plant, called the Camellia sinensis, but the far more commonly consumed black tea is a result of fermented leaves from these plants whereas green tea is from unfermented leaves. Similar to coffee, black tea contains high amounts of caffeine, thus intake should be limited to caffeine consumption of 400 mg. Green and black tea are high in antioxidants while also containing caffeine, making them popular choices for those seeking a boost of energy with a side of health-promoting properties.

Does it work?

Acute caffeine consumption has been shown to speed reaction time in a series of cognitive tests.[14] Black tea has been shown to maintain mental alertness when consumed throughout the day, and this particular study showed no difference in cognitive benefits between black tea and coffee.[15] Epigallocatechin gallate (aka EGCG) is a specific flavonoid of interest in green tea and has been shown superior to placebo in producing a calming effect after a 300 mg dose. [16]

Is it safe?

Green tea contains 30-50 mg of caffeine per 8 oz serving of brewed tea. Black tea contains a bit more caffeine, with about 50 mg in the average brewed cup. Both teas are considered safe when consumed in moderate amounts. As with any caffeinated beverage, it is recommended to limit caffeine intake to 400 mg daily, or 200 mg daily if pregnant/nursing, or have other conditions or take medications which may affect caffeine metabolism. Green tea has been shown to have gastrointestinal side effects when consumed in higher doses.[17]

MATCHA

Sustainability Score: 4/5 Stars

Matcha is a powdered form of green tea, popular in Asian countries, that is prepared in a way to make it stronger than regular teas. Like black and green teas, it also comes from the Camellia sinensis plant. It comes in the form of a finely ground powder and has several uses including giving soba noodles their flavor and green tea ice cream its color. When consumed as a tea it is suspended in water or milk, instead of steeping in a tea bag. Matcha has gained its popularity due to high concentrations of theanine, which is thought to effectively reduce stress. It also contains high concentrations of catechins and polyphenols, antioxidants which have been shown to reduce blood pressure, lower cholesterol, and may even fight against cancer and arthritis.

Does it work?

Research suggests that matcha is superior to placebo in speeding reaction times and improving basic attention 60 minutes after it is consumed.[18] The benefits of theanine are discussed in detail under the section "L-Theanine." But matcha specifically has been shown to reduce stress levels in mice.[19] Additionally, as it is a form of green tea, it is also rich in catechin antioxidants which are thought to aid in weight loss and might even protect against certain types of cancer.

Is it safe?

An 8 oz cup of matcha tea has about 70 mg of caffeine. However, this can vary widely given the various grades of matcha (ceremonial, premium, and cooking grade) as well as ways of preparing it ("thick tea" or "thin tea"). Since matcha has relatively high concentrations of caffeine, the same safety precautions that apply to overconsumption of caffeine apply to matcha.

YERBA MATE

3/5 Stars (for its association with various forms of cancer)

An herbal tea with roots in South America, namely Paraguay, yerba mate, or "mate" for short, has gained popularity worldwide for that extra energy boost. It comes from the leaves of the Ilex paraguariensis tree and is traditionally served in a gourd with a special straw designed to filter out the tiny leaf fragments as it is consumed. You may recall the popular scene from the show *Mozart in the Jungle* where the maestro's assistant diligently watches a video in order to learn how to prepare the maestro's mate just right.

Does it work?

While we know caffeine itself causes increased alertness, more research is needed to demonstrate the cognitive benefits of mate specifically. However, it has been shown to provide a myriad of health benefits including reducing cholesterol, fighting obesity, and protecting against heart disease. However much more research is needed to draw definitive conclusions on these benefits.[20] [21]

Is it safe?

Mate consumption should be limited to short-term use and no more than three cups daily as consuming large amounts for prolonged periods of time has been associated with various forms of cancer including cancer of the lungs, cervix, prostate, gastrointestinal tract, kidney, and bladder.[22]

Yerba mate has approximately 40-50 mg of caffeine per cup. The same precautions that should be taken with all sources of caffeine should be taken with yerba mate.

MACA

Sustainability Score: N/A

Maca, or lepidium meyenii, is a root grown in the Peruvian Andes. When prepared, the dried form is often used as a dietary supplement or can be further processed into flour. It can also be cooked as a root vegetable.

Does it work?

Currently there is no scientific evidence to support the benefits of maca on energy or cognitive function. Some evidence suggests it may be effective in the treatment of sexual dysfunction due to antidepressant therapy, male infertility, and post-menopausal depression/anxiety. [23] [24] [25]

Is it safe?

Maca is considered safe when consumed in food amounts and with continuous use limited to four months or less.

OVERALL CAFFEINE PRECAUTIONS:

Caffeine sources include coffee, tea, chocolate, energy drinks, and even some over-the-counter medications. Too much caffeine intake can lead to symptoms of jitteriness, anxiety, agitation, and diuresis (excess urination). Everyone responds differently to caffeine, and in some, these symptoms can occur with as little as 100 mg of caffeine. Known variables affecting one's sensitivity to caffeine include smoking, age, genetics, pregnancy, and some prescription medications.[26]

Higher doses of caffeine (usually about 1 g) can lead to more severe symptoms of caffeine intoxication, which include rapid or irregular heartbeat, muscle twitching, disorganized thoughts/speech, and in severe cases delirium.[27] Caffeine intoxication can even lead to death with an acute dose of 10-14 grams. [28] [29] Moreover, chronic high dose caffeine intake can lead to tolerance and dependence and with abrupt discontinuation, one can experience withdrawal symptoms including headache, irritability, anxiety, tremor, and concentration difficulties. [30]

The FDA recommends limiting daily caffeine consumption to 400 mg for healthy adults. Those who are pregnant or nursing or who have conditions or take medications altering the metabolism of caffeine should consume no more than 200 mg daily.

CONCLUSION AND OTHER RESOURCES

As you can see, the world beyond coffee is rather extensive, and this book only scratches the surface. When you zoom out, there are basically three buckets of cognitive-enhancing compounds—the first is the bucket of unproven compounds, the second bucket is effective but potentially dangerous, and the third bucket is the scientifically scrutinized compounds that show real and genuine cognitive benefit.

But we would be irresponsible if we did not repeat what we stated at the beginning of this book. Yes, there are a handful of safe, effective, and clinically proven compounds to improve cognitive function (this book alone has hundreds of research citations)—BUT—finding your flow-state is even more dependent on the basics: healthy sleep, healthy diet, regular exercise, and thoughtful stress management. Nootropics and other exogenous compounds come in fifth on this list. And when it comes to trying the supplements, herbs, fungi, and compounds in this book, we recommend you speak with your doctor first. You can bring this book with you.

This is a relatively new category of compounds, and as such it's important to fully research any compounds you are interested in taking.

That said, the current research around nootropics, adaptogens, and mushrooms is clear: it represents an opportunity to create a more personalized self-improvement regime with proven cognitive benefits. And you can design your supplemental stack around a few different cognitive and brain health goals: be they energy management and improvement, mental acuity/attention/focus, emotional stability, decreasing stress, or any combination. Just as we've found in the internet age that information can be personalized, so too can our health habits. Our hope is that this book sparks your own interest down the path of self-improvement, getting into the flow state more easily and more frequently, and finding productivity gains in several areas of life.

For more resources on these compounds and more, visit:

- BeyondCoffeeBook.com for the authors' personal daily regimens, interviews with the authors, free resources (including the first two chapters) to share with friends, and more.
- Reddit.com/r/nootropics is one of the best online communities for learning about this growing realm of compounds.
- *SmartDrugsSmarts* is a favorite podcast and YouTube channel for high-quality research and interviews on cognitive-enhancing compounds.
- Examine.com for free and high-quality summaries on common compounds.
- Amazon.com is our recommended supplier for purchasing supplements in the United States.

ABOUT THE AUTHORS

JAMES BESHARA

James Beshara is a startup founder, advisor, investor, and writer based in San Francisco, California. He has started multiple companies, selling one (Tilt, acquired by Airbnb), and has invested in a number of multibillion-dollar startups. His career has led to (and been a product of) his passion around efficiency, stress management, and productivity. When he was diagnosed with a heart condition in 2013, his doctor introduced him to several compounds as caffeine alternatives. Like many of us, he was surprised by just how much science backs up the cognitive and productivity benefits of nootropics—as opposed to just drinking yet another cup of coffee, as he was accustomed to doing. He has been researching the supplemental world of nootropics for over six years, and what started as a simple blog post for friends has evolved into this comprehensive book. You can follow James on Twitter @jamesbeshara.

DAN ENGLE, MD

Dr. Dan Engle is board certified in psychiatry and neurology. Dr. Engle runs a clinical practice that combines functional medicine, integrative psychiatry, neuro-cognitive restoration, and peak performance methods. He lectures and consults globally and is the medical director of The Revive Treatment Centers of America, as well as medical advisor to several treatment centers that use natural, technological, and medicinal approaches to cognitive healing and recovery. He is a leading expert on cognitive repair. His first book, *The Concussion Repair Manual* published in October 2017, received praise from countless figures in the medical arena. His other programs include B.O.L.D., Freedom From Meds, and Full Spectrum Medicine.

KATHERINE HAYNES, MPAS, PA-C

Katherine Haynes, MPAS, PA-C, is a published medical researcher and physician assistant based in Dallas, Texas. She is a graduate from Vanderbilt University who later obtained her medical training at the University of Texas Southwestern Medical Center in Dallas. She is currently practicing in pediatric neurology, where she actively seeks out natural and less invasive alternatives for her young patients, when appropriate. She is a passionate practitioner of balance, wellness, and mind-body duality, and her experience is directly at the intersection of medical science, research, and the implementation of many compounds that are considered to be nootropics.

NOTES

INTRODUCTION

1   "Is Intermittent Fasting the Key to Improving Cognitive Function ..." 10 Aug. 2017, https://observer.com/2017/08/intermittent-fasting-weight-loss-cognitive-function-health/. Accessed 1 Feb. 2019.

2   "A neurotropic approach to the treatment of multi ... - ScienceDirect.com." https://www.sciencedirect.com/science/article/pii/S0011393X05805181. Accessed 1 Feb. 2019.

CHAPTER ONE: INTRODUCTION TO NOOTROPICS

1   "Establishing Natural Nootropics: Recent Molecular ... - NCBI - NIH." 18 Jul. 2016, https://www.ncbi.nlm.nih.gov/pmc/articles/PMC5021479/. Accessed 18 Feb. 2019.

CHAPTER TWO: POPULAR (AND MOST-RESEARCHED) NOOTROPICS

1   "Association of Serum Docosahexaenoic Acid With Cerebral ... - NCBI." 1 Oct. 2016, https://www.ncbi.nlm.nih.gov/pubmed/27532692. Accessed 20 Feb. 2019.

2   "Phosphatidylserine containing omega-3 fatty acids may ... - NCBI." 3 Jun. 2010, https://www.ncbi.nlm.nih.gov/pubmed/20523044. Accessed 20 Feb. 2019.

3   "12873849 - NCBI - NIH." https://www.ncbi.nlm.nih.gov/pubmed/12873849. Accessed 20 Feb. 2019.

4   "B-vitamins and fatty acids in the prevention and treatment of ... - NCBI." https://www.ncbi.nlm.nih.gov/pubmed/20847412. Accessed 20 Feb. 2019.

5   "Effect of n-3 PUFA supplementation on cognitive function ... - NCBI." 15 Oct. 2014, https://www.ncbi.nlm.nih.gov/pubmed/25411277. Accessed 20 Feb. 2019.

6   "Docosahexaenoic acid and adult memory: a systematic review - NCBI." 18 Mar. 2015, https://www.ncbi.nlm.nih.gov/pubmed/25786262. Accessed 20 Feb. 2019.

7   "Effects of ω-3 fatty acids on cognitive performance: a meta ... - NCBI." 3 Feb. 2012, https://www.ncbi.nlm.nih.gov/pubmed/22305186. Accessed 20 Feb. 2019.

8   "Omega-3 Polyunsaturated Fatty Acids in Youths with Attention ... - NCBI." 25 Jul. 2017, https://www.ncbi.nlm.nih.gov/pubmed/28741625. Accessed 20 Feb. 2019.

9   https://ods.od.nih.gov/factsheets/Omega3FattyAcids-HealthProfessional/#cardiovascular

10   "Role of omega-3 fatty acids in the treatment of depressive ... - NCBI." https://www.ncbi.nlm.nih.gov/pubmed/24805797. Accessed 23 Feb. 2019.

11   https://ods.od.nih.gov/factsheets/Omega3FattyAcids-HealthProfessional/#h8

12   "Changes in the interaction between CNS cholinergic and ... - NCBI." https://www.ncbi.nlm.nih.gov/pubmed/3709792. Accessed 20 Feb. 2019.

13   https://www.ncbi.nlm.nih.gov/pmc/articles/PMC4595381/

14   https://www.sciencedirect.com/science/article/pii/S0011393X05805181

15   https://jissn.biomedcentral.com/articles/10.1186/1550-2783-5-S1-P15

16   "GRAS Notice 000419: L-alpha-glycerylphosphorylcholine - NooCube." https://cdn.noocube.com/wp-content/uploads/2015/12/09152523/NooCube-AlphaGPC3.pdf. Accessed 20 Feb. 2019.

17   "Changes in brain striatum dopamine and acetylcholine ... - NCBI - NIH." https://www.ncbi.nlm.nih.gov/pmc/articles/PMC1908237/. Accessed 20 Feb. 2019.

18 "Changes in brain biogenic monoamines induced by the nootropic" http://europepmc.org/abstract/med/2105261. Accessed 20 Feb. 2019.

19 "Cytidine(5')diphosphocholine enhances the ability of ... - NCBI." https://www.ncbi.nlm.nih.gov/pubmed/6543245. Accessed 20 Feb. 2019.

20 https://www.ncbi.nlm.nih.gov/pmc/articles/PMC4562749/

21 "The Effect of Citicoline Supplementation on Motor Speed and ... - NCBI." 15 Jul. 2015, https://www.ncbi.nlm.nih.gov/pubmed/26179181. Accessed 20 Feb. 2019.

22 "Treatment of postconcussional symptoms with CDP-choline. - NCBI." https://www.ncbi.nlm.nih.gov/pubmed/1940965. Accessed 20 Feb. 2019.

23 https://www.ncbi.nlm.nih.gov/pubmed/11079534

24 https://www.nutraingredients.com/Article/2014/07/18/Citicoline-wins-EU-novel-foods-approval-in-medical-foods-and-food-supplements

25 "The neuropharmacology of L-theanine(N-ethyl-L-glutamine): a ... - NCBI." https://www.ncbi.nlm.nih.gov/pubmed/17182482. Accessed 20 Feb. 2019.

26 "Inhibition by theanine of binding of [3H]AMPA, [3H]kainate, and ... - NCBI." https://www.ncbi.nlm.nih.gov/pubmed/12596867. Accessed 20 Feb. 2019.

27 https://www.webmd.com/vitamins/ai/ingredientmono-1053/theanine

28 "Acute effects of theanine, caffeine and theanine-caffeine ... - NCBI." 12 Feb. 2016, https://www.ncbi.nlm.nih.gov/pubmed/26869148. Accessed 20 Feb. 2019.

29 "Acute effects of tea constituents L-theanine, caffeine, and ... - NCBI." 19 Jun. 2014, https://www.ncbi.nlm.nih.gov/pubmed/24946991. Accessed 20 Feb. 2019.

30 "A combination of green tea extract and l-theanine improves ... - NCBI." 8 Feb. 2011, https://www.ncbi.nlm.nih.gov/pubmed/21303262. Accessed 20 Feb. 2019.

31 "The effects of L-theanine (Suntheanine®) on objective sleep ... - NCBI." https://www.ncbi.nlm.nih.gov/pubmed/22214254. Accessed 20 Feb. 2019.

32 "Effects of chronic l-theanine administration in patients with ... - NCBI." 11 Jul. 2016, https://www.ncbi.nlm.nih.gov/pubmed/27396868. Accessed 20 Feb. 2019.

33 https://www.sciencedirect.com/science/article/pii/S2352385915003138?via%3Dihub

34 "Effects of L-theanine or caffeine intake on changes in blood ... - NCBI." 29 Oct. 2012, https://www.ncbi.nlm.nih.gov/pubmed/23107346. Accessed 20 Feb. 2019.

35 "The acute effects of L-theanine in comparison with alprazolam ... - NCBI." https://www.ncbi.nlm.nih.gov/pubmed/15378679. Accessed 20 Feb. 2019.

36 https://en.wikipedia.org/wiki/Theanine

37 "A prospective, randomized double-blind ..." https://www.ncbi.nlm.nih.gov/pubmed/23439798. Accessed 23 Feb. 2019.

38 "Naturopathic care for anxiety: a randomized controlled trial - NCBI." 31 Aug. 2009, https://www.ncbi.nlm.nih.gov/pubmed/19718255. Accessed 23 Feb. 2019.

39 "Khyati S. And Thaker Anup: Randomized Double Blind Placebo ... - IAMJ." http://www.iamj.in/images/upload/01.05.14_IAMJ.pdf. Accessed 23 Feb. 2019.

40 https://en.wikipedia.org/wiki/Bacopa_monnieri#Traditional_uses

41 "The chronic effects of an extract of Bacopa monniera (Brahmi) - NCBI." https://www.ncbi.nlm.nih.gov/pubmed/11498727. Accessed 24 Feb. 2019.

42 "Chronic effects of Brahmi (Bacopa monnieri) on human memory. - NCBI." https://www.ncbi.nlm.nih.gov/pubmed/12093601. Accessed 24 Feb. 2019.

43 "Does Bacopa monnieri improve memory performance in older ... - NCBI." https://www.ncbi.nlm.nih.gov/pubmed/20590480. Accessed 24 Feb. 2019.

44 "Meta-analysis of randomized controlled trials on cognitive ... - NCBI." 16 Nov. 2018, https://www.ncbi.nlm.nih.gov/pubmed/24252493. Accessed 24 Feb. 2019.

45 "An acute, double-blind, placebo-controlled cross-over study of ... - NCBI." 21 Jun. 2013, https://www.ncbi.nlm.nih.gov/pubmed/23788517. Accessed 24 Feb. 2019.

46 "bacopa monniera(l.) pennell - European Journal of Pharmaceutical ..." 29 Jun. 2016, https://www.ejpmr.com/admin/assets/article_issue/1469866819.pdf. Accessed 24 Feb. 2019.

47 "An open-label study to elucidate the effects of standardized ... - NCBI." https://www.ncbi.nlm.nih.gov/pubmed/24682000. Accessed 24 Feb. 2019.

48 https://www.ncbi.nlm.nih.gov/pubmed/10230711

49 "The effects of dietary neurotransmitter precursors on ... - NCBI - NIH." https://www.ncbi.nlm.nih.gov/pubmed/4025206. Accessed 27 Feb. 2019.

50 https://www.ncbi.nlm.nih.gov/pubmed/2736402

51 https://www.ncbi.nlm.nih.gov/pubmed/7794222

52 https://www.webmd.com/vitamins/ai/ingredientmono-1037/tyrosine

53 "Biochemical changes of rat brain membranes with aging - Springer Link." https://link.springer.com/article/10.1007/BF00965104. Accessed 27 Feb. 2019.

54 "Cognitive decline in the elderly: a double-blind, placebo ... - NCBI." https://www.ncbi.nlm.nih.gov/pubmed/8323999. Accessed 27 Feb. 2019.

55 "Effects of phosphatidylserine in age-associated memory ... - NCBI." https://www.ncbi.nlm.nih.gov/pubmed/2027477. Accessed 27 Feb. 2019.

56 "Peer-Reviewed Studies & Health References | 19 - Truth Nutra." https://www.truthnutra.com/pages/references?page=19&q=anabolicmen. Accessed 27 Feb. 2019.

57 "Phosphatidylserine containing omega-3 Fatty acids may ... - NCBI." 20 Feb. 2018, https://www.ncbi.nlm.nih.gov/pubmed/24577097. Accessed 27 Feb. 2019.

58 "The effect of phosphatidylserine administration on memory and ... - NCBI." 17 Mar. 2013, https://www.ncbi.nlm.nih.gov/pubmed/23495677. Accessed 27 Feb. 2019.

59 "Caffeine - Wikipedia." https://en.wikipedia.org/wiki/Caffeine. Accessed 27 Feb. 2019.

60 "Treatment of severe, disabling migraine attacks in an over-the ... - NCBI." https://www.ncbi.nlm.nih.gov/pubmed/10524663. Accessed 27 Feb. 2019.

61 "Efficacy and safety of acetaminophen, aspirin, and caffeine in ... - NCBI." https://www.ncbi.nlm.nih.gov/pubmed/9482363. Accessed 27 Feb. 2019.

62 "Oral sumatriptan for acute migraine. - NCBI." https://www.ncbi.nlm.nih.gov/pubmed/12917936. Accessed 27 Feb. 2019.

63 "Efficacy of diclofenac sodium softgel 100 mg with or without ... - NCBI." https://www.ncbi.nlm.nih.gov/pubmed/14756851. Accessed 27 Feb. 2019.

64 "Caffeine as an analgesic adjuvant in tension headache. - NCBI." https://www.ncbi.nlm.nih.gov/pubmed/7955822. Accessed 27 Feb. 2019.

65 "The fixed combination of acetylsalicylic acid, paracetamol and ... - NCBI." https://www.ncbi.nlm.nih.gov/pubmed/16162254. Accessed 27 Feb. 2019.

66 "The effects of black tea and other beverages on aspects of ... - NCBI." https://www.ncbi.nlm.nih.gov/pubmed/9784078. Accessed 27 Feb. 2019.

67 "Effects of caffeine on alertness as measured by infrared ... - NCBI." 9 Jun. 2008, https://www.ncbi.nlm.nih.gov/pubmed/18537025. Accessed 27 Feb. 2019.

68 "Comparing the benefits of caffeine, naps and placebo on ... - NCBI - NIH." 8 May. 2008, https://www.ncbi.nlm.nih.gov/pubmed/18554731. Accessed 27 Feb. 2019.

69 "Effects of 2 adenosine antagonists, quercetin and caffeine, on ... - NCBI." https://www.ncbi.nlm.nih.gov/pubmed/20814335. Accessed 27 Feb. 2019.

70 "The effects of a low dose of caffeine on cognitive performance. - NCBI." https://www.ncbi.nlm.nih.gov/pubmed/9862410. Accessed 27 Feb. 2019.

71 "Using coffee to compensate for poor sleep: Impact on vigilance ... - NCBI." 20 Mar. 2018, https://www.ncbi.nlm.nih.gov/pubmed/29866304. Accessed 1 Mar. 2019.

72 "18006208 - NCBI." https://www.ncbi.nlm.nih.gov/pubmed/18006208. Accessed 27 Feb. 2019.

73 "The Science – Future Nutrients." https://futurenutrients.co.nz/the-science/. Accessed 1 Mar. 2019.

74 "L-theanine and caffeine improve task switching but not ... - NCBI." 15 Jan. 2010, https://www.ncbi.nlm.nih.gov/pubmed/20079786. Accessed 1 Mar. 2019.

75 "The combination of L-theanine and caffeine improves cognitive ... - NCBI." https://www.ncbi.nlm.nih.gov/pubmed/21040626. Accessed 1 Mar. 2019.

76 "Assessing the effects of caffeine and theanine on the ... - NCBI." 2 Feb. 2012, https://www.ncbi.nlm.nih.gov/pubmed/22326943. Accessed 1 Mar. 2019.

77 "Caffeine, extraversion and working memory. - NCBI." 26 Sep. 2012, https://www.ncbi.nlm.nih.gov/pubmed/23015541. Accessed 1 Mar. 2019.

78 "Caffeine's effects on true and false memory. - NCBI." https://www.ncbi.nlm.nih.gov/pubmed/19708406. Accessed 1 Mar. 2019.

79 "Relationships Between Caffeine Intake and Risk for ... - NCBI - NIH." 27 Sep. 2016, https://www.ncbi.nlm.nih.gov/pubmed/27678290. Accessed 1 Mar. 2019.

80 "Caffeine and cognitive decline in elderly women at high ... - NCBI - NIH." https://www.ncbi.nlm.nih.gov/pubmed/23422357. Accessed 1 Mar. 2019.

81 "Acute Rhodiola rosea intake can improve endurance exercise ... - NCBI." https://www.ncbi.nlm.nih.gov/pubmed/15256690. Accessed 4 Mar. 2019.

82 "The effects of an acute dose of Rhodiola rosea on endurance ... - NCBI." https://www.ncbi.nlm.nih.gov/pubmed/23443221. Accessed 4 Mar. 2019.

83 "Effects of chronic Rhodiola Rosea supplementation on sport ... - NCBI." https://www.ncbi.nlm.nih.gov/pubmed/20308973. Accessed 4 Mar. 2019.

84 "Effects of chronic Rhodiola Rosea supplementation on sport ... - NCBI." https://www.ncbi.nlm.nih.gov/pubmed/20308973. Accessed 4 Mar. 2019.

85 "Evaluation of Rhodiola rosea supplementation on skeletal ... - NCBI." 18 Sep. 2013, https://www.ncbi.nlm.nih.gov/pubmed/24055627. Accessed 4 Mar. 2019.

86 "Clinical trial of Rhodiola rosea L. extract SHR-5 in the treatment ... - NCBI." https://www.ncbi.nlm.nih.gov/pubmed/17990195. Accessed 4 Mar. 2019.

87 "A pilot study of Rhodiola rosea (Rhodax) for generalized ... - NCBI." https://www.ncbi.nlm.nih.gov/pubmed/18307390. Accessed 4 Mar. 2019.

88 "Therapeutic effects and safety of Rhodiola rosea extract WS ... - NCBI." 6 Jan. 2012, https://www.ncbi.nlm.nih.gov/pubmed/22228617. Accessed 4 Mar. 2019.

89 "A double-blind, placebo-controlled pilot study of the stimulating ... - NCBI." https://www.ncbi.nlm.nih.gov/pubmed/10839209. Accessed 4 Mar. 2019.

90 "Rhodiola rosea in stress induced fatigue--a double blind cross ... - NCBI." https://www.ncbi.nlm.nih.gov/pubmed/11081987. Accessed 4 Mar. 2019.

91 "A randomized trial of two different doses of a SHR-5 Rhodiola ... - NCBI." https://www.ncbi.nlm.nih.gov/pubmed/12725561. Accessed 4 Mar. 2019.

92 "Panax ginseng enhances cognitive performance in Alzheimer ... - NCBI." https://www.ncbi.nlm.nih.gov/pubmed/18580589. Accessed 9 Mar. 2019.

93 "Improved cognitive performance in human volunteers following ... - NCBI." https://www.ncbi.nlm.nih.gov/pubmed/15582012. Accessed 9 Mar. 2019.

94 "Efficacy and safety of the standardised Ginseng extract G115 - NCBI." https://www.ncbi.nlm.nih.gov/pubmed/8879982. Accessed 9 Mar. 2019.

95 "Antifatigue effects of Panax ginseng CA Meyer: a randomised ... - NCBI." 17 Apr.
2013, https://www.ncbi.nlm.nih.gov/pubmed/23613825. Accessed 9 Mar. 2019.

96 "The effects of acute doses of standardized Ginkgo biloba ... - NCBI." https://www.
ncbi.nlm.nih.gov/pubmed/10441781. Accessed 18 Mar. 2019.

97 "Is Ginkgo biloba a cognitive enhancer in healthy individuals? A ... - NCBI." https://
www.ncbi.nlm.nih.gov/pubmed/23001963. Accessed 18 Mar. 2019.

98 "Ginkgo biloba for cognitive impairment and dementia. - NCBI." https://www.ncbi.
nlm.nih.gov/pubmed/12519586. Accessed 18 Mar. 2019.

99 "Efficacy and tolerability of a once daily formulation of Ginkgo ... - NCBI." 15 Nov.
2018, https://www.ncbi.nlm.nih.gov/pubmed/22086747. Accessed 18 Mar. 2019.

100 "Ginkgo biloba compared with cholinesterase inhibitors in the treatment ..." https://
www.ncbi.nlm.nih.gov/pubmed/15237280. Accessed 18 Mar. 2019.

101 "Efficacy of rivastigmine in comparison to ginkgo for treating ... - NCBI." https://
www.ncbi.nlm.nih.gov/pubmed/23866514. Accessed 18 Mar. 2019.

102 "Ginkgo biloba for prevention of dementia: a randomized controlled trial.." https://
www.ncbi.nlm.nih.gov/pubmed/19017911. Accessed 18 Mar. 2019.

103 "Ginkgo biloba for preventing cognitive decline in older ... - NCBI - NIH." 23 Dec.
2009, https://www.ncbi.nlm.nih.gov/pubmed/20040554. Accessed 18 Mar. 2019.

104 "Ginkgo biloba special extract EGb 761 in generalized anxiety disorder ..." 30 Jun.
2006, https://www.ncbi.nlm.nih.gov/pubmed/16808927. Accessed 18 Mar. 2019.

105 "Comparison of two dosages of ginkgo biloba extract EGb 761 ... - NCBI." https://
www.ncbi.nlm.nih.gov/pubmed/10604042. Accessed 18 Mar. 2019.

106 "Effect of Ginkgo Biloba (EGb 761) on Treadmill Walking ... - NCBI - NIH." https://
www.ncbi.nlm.nih.gov/pmc/articles/PMC2748261/. Accessed 18 Mar. 2019.

107 "TR-578 Toxicology and Carcinogenesis Studies of Ginkgo biloba Extract." 1 Dec.
2005, https://ntp.niehs.nih.gov/go/tr578. Accessed 15 Mar. 2019.

108 "Occurrence of neurotoxic 4'-O-methylpyridoxine in Ginkgo biloba ..." https://www.
ncbi.nlm.nih.gov/pubmed/17252495. Accessed 18 Mar. 2019.

CHAPTER THREE: UNSUSTAINABLE NOOTROPICS

1   "Does nicotine cause cancer? - European Code Against Cancer - iarc." https://cancer-code-europe.iarc.fr/index.php/en/ecac-12-ways/tobacco/199-nicotine-cause-cancer. Accessed 24 Mar. 2019.

2   "Electronic cigarettes. A position statement of the forum of ... - NCBI." 15 Sep. 2014, https://www.ncbi.nlm.nih.gov/pubmed/25006874. Accessed 24 Mar. 2019.

3   "Why all stimulant drugs are damaging to recreational users: an ... - NCBI." https://www.ncbi.nlm.nih.gov/pubmed/26216554. Accessed 24 Mar. 2019.

4   "The scientific case that nicotine is addictive. - NCBI." https://www.ncbi.nlm.nih.gov/pubmed/7724697. Accessed 24 Mar. 2019.

5   "Nicotine replacement therapy for smoking cessation. - NCBI." 14 Nov. 2012, https://www.ncbi.nlm.nih.gov/pubmed/23152200. Accessed 24 Mar. 2019.

6   "[Psychiatric and psychological features of nicotine dependence]. - NCBI." https://www.ncbi.nlm.nih.gov/pubmed/23631239. Accessed 24 Mar. 2019.

7   "Nicotine and Tobacco as Substances of Abuse in Children and ... - NCBI." https://www.ncbi.nlm.nih.gov/pubmed/27994114. Accessed 24 Mar. 2019.

8   "The effects of nicotine on human fetal development. - NCBI." 13 Jun. 2016, https://www.ncbi.nlm.nih.gov/pubmed/27297020. Accessed 24 Mar. 2019.

9   "How much nicotine kills a human? Tracing back the generally ... - NCBI." 4 Oct. 2013, https://www.ncbi.nlm.nih.gov/pubmed/24091634. Accessed 24 Mar. 2019.

10 "Nicotine - The Health Consequences of Smoking—50 ... - NCBI - NIH." https://www.ncbi.nlm.nih.gov/books/NBK294308/. Accessed 24 Mar. 2019.

11 https://www.ncbi.nlm.nih.gov/pubmed/11869656

12 https://www.ncbi.nlm.nih.gov/pubmed/9802912

13 https://www.ncbi.nlm.nih.gov/pubmed/3536521

14 https://www.ncbi.nlm.nih.gov/pubmed/2468734

15 https://medlineplus.gov/druginfo/natural/794.html

16 https://bebrainfit.com/too-much-serotonin/

17   https://www.ncbi.nlm.nih.gov/pubmed/25499957

18   https://www.ncbi.nlm.nih.gov/pubmed/25591060

19   https://www.webmd.com/add-adhd/adderall-withdrawal#1

20   https://www.webmd.com/drugs/2/drug-3670-6080/dextroamphetamine-
      amphetamine-oral/dextroamphetamine-amphetamine-oral/
      details

21   https://www.ncbi.nlm.nih.gov/pubmed/29502274

22   https://www.ncbi.nlm.nih.gov/pubmed/22070796

23   http://www.racetam.org/aniracetam-side-effects/

24   "Valproic acid overdose and L-carnitine therapy. - NCBI." https://www.ncbi.nlm.
      nih.gov/pubmed/8837953. Accessed 23 Mar. 2019.

25   "Carnitine supplementation for inborn errors of metabolism. - NCBI." 15 Feb. 2012,
      https://www.ncbi.nlm.nih.gov/pubmed/22336821. Accessed 23 Mar. 2019.

26   "Effects of prolonged L-carnitine administration on delayed muscle pain ..." https://
      www.ncbi.nlm.nih.gov/pubmed/8858401. Accessed 23 Mar. 2019.

27   "The effects of acute L-carnitine supplementation on endurance ... - NCBI." https://
      www.ncbi.nlm.nih.gov/pubmed/24263659. Accessed 23 Mar. 2019.

28   "Effects of L-carnitine supplementation on physical performance ... - NCBI." https://
      www.ncbi.nlm.nih.gov/pubmed/8803503. Accessed 23 Mar. 2019.

29   "The effects of L-carnitine supplementation on performance during ..." https://www.
      ncbi.nlm.nih.gov/pubmed/8063466. Accessed 23 Mar. 2019.

30   "Effects of Citric Acid and l-Carnitine on Physical Fatigue. - NCBI." https://www.
      ncbi.nlm.nih.gov/pubmed/18299720. Accessed 23 Mar. 2019.

31   "The influence on cognition of the interactions between lecithin ... - NCBI." https://
      www.ncbi.nlm.nih.gov/pubmed/14760514. Accessed 23 Mar. 2019.

32   "A prospective double-blind, randomized clinical trial of ... - NCBI." https://www.
      ncbi.nlm.nih.gov/pubmed/21629200. Accessed 23 Mar. 2019.

33   "Efficacy of carnitine in the treatment of children with attention ... - NCBI." https://www.ncbi.nlm.nih.gov/pubmed/12213433. Accessed 23 Mar. 2019.

34   https://ods.od.nih.gov/factsheets/Carnitine-HealthProfessional/#h7

35   https://www.ncbi.nlm.nih.gov/pmc/articles/PMC3407788/

36   https://www.webmd.com/diet/supplement-guide-creatine#1-5

37   https://www.ncbi.nlm.nih.gov/pmc/articles/PMC4063424/

38   Ibid.

39   https://www.ncbi.nlm.nih.gov/pmc/articles/PMC2328349/pdf/canfamphys00038-0075.pdf

40   https://www.alz.org/media/Documents/fda-approved-treatments-alzheimers-ts.pdf

41   https://www.webmd.com/drugs/2/drug-14334-9218/donepezil-oral/donepezil-oral/details

42   https://www.ncbi.nlm.nih.gov/pubmed/24086396

43   "Huperzine-A capsules enhance memory and learning ... - NCBI." https://www.ncbi.nlm.nih.gov/pubmed/10678121. Accessed 23 Mar. 2019.

44   "Huperzine A for mild cognitive impairment (Review) - Cochrane Library." https://www.cochranelibrary.com/cdsr/doi/10.1002/14651858.CD008827.pub2/epdf/full. Accessed 23 Mar. 2019.

45   https://www.webmd.com/vitamins/ai/ingredientmono-764/huperzine-a

46   "Label (PDF) - FDA." https://www.accessdata.fda.gov/drugsatfda_docs/label/2008/019334s019s020lbl.pdf. Accessed 23 Mar. 2019.

47   "Monoamine oxidase type B inhibitors in early Parkinson's ... - NCBI - NIH." 6 Jul. 2004, https://www.ncbi.nlm.nih.gov/pmc/articles/PMC516655/. Accessed 23 Mar. 2019.

48   "Placing transdermal selegiline for major ... - ScienceDirect.com." https://www.sciencedirect.com/science/article/pii/S0165032713005077. Accessed 23 Mar. 2019.

49   https://www.ncbi.nlm.nih.gov/pubmed/15661631

50   https://www.ncbi.nlm.nih.gov/pubmed/30684794

51   "Use of cognitive enhancers: methylphenidate and analogs. - NCBI." https://www.
     ncbi.nlm.nih.gov/pubmed/30657540. Accessed 23 Mar. 2019.

52   https://www.ncbi.nlm.nih.gov/
     pubmed?Db=pubmed&Cmd=ShowDetailView&TermToSearch=10907387

53   "Reference ID: 3685660 - FDA." https://www.accessdata.fda.gov/drugsatfda_docs/
     label/2015/020717s037s038lbl.pdf. Accessed 23 Mar. 2019.

54   "Modafinil for cognitive neuroenhancement in healthy non-sleep ... - NCBI." 20 Aug.
     2015, https://www.ncbi.nlm.nih.gov/pubmed/26381811. Accessed 23 Mar. 2019.

55   https://www.ncbi.nlm.nih.gov/pubmed/11830761

56   https://www.ncbi.nlm.nih.gov/pubmed/29265084

57   https://thedrugclassroom.com/video/phenibut/

58   https://www.webmd.com/vitamins/ai/ingredientmono-1184/phenibut

59   https://www.ncbi.nlm.nih.gov/pubmed/1794001

60   "The clinical safety of high-dose piracetam--its use in the ... - NCBI." https://www.
     ncbi.nlm.nih.gov/pubmed/10338106. Accessed 23 Mar. 2019.

61   "Piracetam for dementia or cognitive impairment. - NCBI." https://www.ncbi.nlm.
     nih.gov/pubmed/11405971. Accessed 23 Mar. 2019.

62   "Clinical efficacy of piracetam in cognitive impairment: a meta ... - NCBI." https://
     www.ncbi.nlm.nih.gov/pubmed/12006732. Accessed 23 Mar. 2019.

63   "Piracetam: a review of pharmacological properties and clinical ... - NCBI." https://
     www.ncbi.nlm.nih.gov/pubmed/16007238. Accessed 23 Mar. 2019.

CHAPTER FOUR: ADAPTOGENS, MUSHROOMS, AND ANTI-INFLAMMATORIES

1   "Effect of the Indian gooseberry (amla) on serum cholesterol levels in ..." https://
     www.ncbi.nlm.nih.gov/pubmed/3250870. Accessed 18 Mar. 2019.

2   "Double-blind, placebo-controlled pilot and phase III study of activity of ..." https://
      www.ncbi.nlm.nih.gov/pubmed/11081985. Accessed 18 Mar. 2019.

3   "The effect of eight weeks of supplementation with Eleutherococcus ..." https://
      www.ncbi.nlm.nih.gov/pubmed/21793317. Accessed 18 Mar. 2019.

4   "Double-blind, placebo-controlled, randomised study of single dose ..." 5 Apr. 2010,
      https://www.ncbi.nlm.nih.gov/pubmed/20374974. Accessed 18 Mar. 2019.

5   "No benefit adding eleutherococcus senticosus to stress management ..." 5 Jun. 2013,
      https://www.ncbi.nlm.nih.gov/pubmed/23740477. Accessed 18 Mar. 2019.

6   https://www.ncbi.nlm.nih.gov/pubmed/17924700

7   "Controlled programmed trial of Ocimum sanctum leaf on ... - NCBI." https://www.
      ncbi.nlm.nih.gov/pubmed/19253862. Accessed 21 Mar. 2019.

8   "Antifertility screening of plants. 3. Effect of six indigenous plants on ..." https://
      www.ncbi.nlm.nih.gov/pubmed/5820437. Accessed 9 Mar. 2019.

9   "Reversible anti-fertility effect of benzene extract of Ocimum ... - NCBI." https://
      www.ncbi.nlm.nih.gov/pubmed/12099405. Accessed 9 Mar. 2019.

10   https://www.ncbi.nlm.nih.gov/pubmed/27621241

11   "A double-blind placebo-controlled trial of maca root as ... - NCBI." 14 Apr. 2015,
      https://www.ncbi.nlm.nih.gov/pubmed/25954318. Accessed 21 Mar. 2019.

12   https://www.ncbi.nlm.nih.gov/pubmed/20691074

13   "Acute Rhodiola rosea intake can improve endurance exercise ... - NCBI." https://
      www.ncbi.nlm.nih.gov/pubmed/15256690. Accessed 4 Mar. 2019.

14   "The effects of an acute dose of Rhodiola rosea on endurance ... - NCBI." https://
      www.ncbi.nlm.nih.gov/pubmed/23443221. Accessed 4 Mar. 2019.

15   "Effects of chronic Rhodiola Rosea supplementation on sport ... - NCBI." https://
      www.ncbi.nlm.nih.gov/pubmed/20308973. Accessed 4 Mar. 2019.

16   "Effects of chronic Rhodiola Rosea supplementation on sport ... - NCBI." https://
      www.ncbi.nlm.nih.gov/pubmed/20308973. Accessed 4 Mar. 2019.

17   "Evaluation of Rhodiola rosea supplementation on skeletal ... - NCBI." 18 Sep. 2013,
      https://www.ncbi.nlm.nih.gov/pubmed/24055627. Accessed 4 Mar. 2019.

18 "Clinical trial of Rhodiola rosea L. extract SHR-5 in the treatment ... - NCBI." https://www.ncbi.nlm.nih.gov/pubmed/17990195. Accessed 4 Mar. 2019.

19 "A pilot study of Rhodiola rosea (Rhodax) for generalized ... - NCBI." https://www.ncbi.nlm.nih.gov/pubmed/18307390. Accessed 4 Mar. 2019.

20 "Therapeutic effects and safety of Rhodiola rosea extract WS ... - NCBI." 6 Jan. 2012, https://www.ncbi.nlm.nih.gov/pubmed/22228617. Accessed 4 Mar. 2019.

21 "A double-blind, placebo-controlled pilot study of the stimulating ... - NCBI." https://www.ncbi.nlm.nih.gov/pubmed/10839209. Accessed 4 Mar. 2019.

22 "Rhodiola rosea in stress induced fatigue--a double blind cross ... - NCBI." https://www.ncbi.nlm.nih.gov/pubmed/11081987. Accessed 4 Mar. 2019.

23 "A randomized trial of two different doses of a SHR-5 Rhodiola ... - NCBI." https://www.ncbi.nlm.nih.gov/pubmed/12725561. Accessed 4 Mar. 2019.

24 "A prospective, randomized double-blind ..." https://www.ncbi.nlm.nih.gov/pubmed/23439798. Accessed 23 Feb. 2019.

25 "Naturopathic care for anxiety: a randomized controlled trial - NCBI." 31 Aug. 2009, https://www.ncbi.nlm.nih.gov/pubmed/19718255. Accessed 23 Feb. 2019.

26 "Khyati S. And Thaker Anup: Randomized Double Blind Placebo ... - IAMJ." http://www.iamj.in/images/upload/01.05.14_IAMJ.pdf. Accessed 23 Feb. 2019.

27 "Neurotrophic properties of the Lion's mane medicinal mushroom - NCBI." https://www.ncbi.nlm.nih.gov/pubmed/24266378. Accessed 21 Mar. 2019.

28 "The Neuroprotective Properties of Hericium erinaceus in Glutamate ..." 1 Nov. 2016, https://www.ncbi.nlm.nih.gov/pubmed/27809277. Accessed 21 Mar. 2019.

29 "High molecular weight of polysaccharides from Hericium erinaceus ..." https://www.ncbi.nlm.nih.gov/pubmed/27266872. Accessed 21 Mar. 2019.

30 "Gastroprotective Effects of Lion's Mane Mushroom Hericium erinaceus ..." 5 Nov. 2013, https://www.ncbi.nlm.nih.gov/pubmed/24302966. Accessed 21 Mar. 2019.

31 "Protective Effect of Ethanol Extracts of Hericium erinaceus on Alloxan ..." 29 Aug. 2014, https://www.ncbi.nlm.nih.gov/pmc/articles/PMC4415746/. Accessed 21 Mar. 2019.

32   "Immunomodulatory Activities of a Fungal Protein Extracted from ... - NCBI." 12 Jun. 2017, https://www.ncbi.nlm.nih.gov/pubmed/28713364. Accessed 21 Mar. 2019.

33   "Improving effects of the mushroom Yamabushitake (Hericium erinaceus)." https://www.ncbi.nlm.nih.gov/pubmed/18844328. Accessed 21 Mar. 2019.

34   "Reduction of depression and anxiety by 4 weeks Hericium erinaceus ..." https://www.ncbi.nlm.nih.gov/pubmed/20834180. Accessed 21 Mar. 2019.

35   https://www.ncbi.nlm.nih.gov/pubmed/15588653

36   https://www.ncbi.nlm.nih.gov/pmc/articles/PMC4946216/

37   https://ieeexplore.ieee.org/document/5305591

38   https://www.ncbi.nlm.nih.gov/pubmed/23280601

39   https://www.liebertpub.com/doi/abs/10.1089/jmf.2012.0222

40   "Effect of Maitake (Grifola frondosa) D-Fraction on the activation ... - NCBI." https://www.ncbi.nlm.nih.gov/pubmed/14977447. Accessed 21 Mar. 2019.

41   https://www.ncbi.nlm.nih.gov/pubmed/25704018

42   "Role of curcumin in systemic and oral health: An overview. - NCBI." https://www.ncbi.nlm.nih.gov/pubmed/23633828. Accessed 22 Mar. 2019.

43   "Antifungal activity of turmeric oil extracted from Curcuma longa - NCBI." https://www.ncbi.nlm.nih.gov/pubmed/8824742. Accessed 22 Mar. 2019.

44   "Anti-inflammatory properties of curcumin, a major constituent. - NCBI." https://www.ncbi.nlm.nih.gov/pubmed/19594223. Accessed 22 Mar. 2019.

45   "Phase II clinical trial on effect of the long turmeric (Curcuma longa Linn ..." https://www.ncbi.nlm.nih.gov/pubmed/11485087. Accessed 22 Mar. 2019.

46   "Efficacy and safety of curcumin in major depressive disorder: a ... - NCBI." https://www.ncbi.nlm.nih.gov/pubmed/23832433. Accessed 22 Mar. 2019.

47   https://www.ncbi.nlm.nih.gov/pmc/articles/PMC3995184/

48   https://www.ncbi.nlm.nih.gov/pubmed/20842754

49   https://www.ncbi.nlm.nih.gov/pubmed/21031618

50 https://www.ncbi.nlm.nih.gov/pmc/articles/PMC4277626/

51 https://www.ncbi.nlm.nih.gov/pubmed/23754631

52 "Effects of dietary Spirulina on vascular reactivity. - NCBI." https://www.ncbi.nlm.
    nih.gov/pubmed/19298191. Accessed 22 Mar. 2019.

53 https://www.ncbi.nlm.nih.gov/pubmed/20010119

CHAPTER FIVE: MORE ON COFFEE AND COFFEE ALTERNATIVES

1   "Dose-dependent pharmacokinetics and psychomotor ... - NCBI - NIH." https://
    www.ncbi.nlm.nih.gov/pubmed/9378841. Accessed 27 Jun. 2019.

2   "Caffeine-related atrial fibrillation. - NCBI." https://www.ncbi.nlm.nih.gov/
    pubmed/20634688. Accessed 25 Jun. 2019.

3   "Coffee consumption is not associated with increased risk of ... - NCBI." 23 Sep. 2015,
    https://www.ncbi.nlm.nih.gov/pmc/articles/PMC4579587/. Accessed 24 Jun. 2019.

4   "Does Caffeine Consumption Increase the Risk of New-Onset ... - NCBI." 2 Jul. 2018,
    https://www.ncbi.nlm.nih.gov/pubmed/29966128. Accessed 24 Jun. 2019.

5   "A survey of physician advice about caffeine. - NCBI - NIH." https://www.ncbi.nlm.
    nih.gov/pubmed/2485281. Accessed 25 Jun. 2019.

6   "Caffeine Stimulation of Cortisol Secretion Across the Waking ... - NCBI." https://
    www.ncbi.nlm.nih.gov/pmc/articles/PMC2257922/. Accessed 24 Jun. 2019.

7   "In Summary: Caffeine for the Sustainment of Mental Task Performance ..." https://
    www.ncbi.nlm.nih.gov/pubmed/11984428. Accessed 25 Jun. 2019.

8   "Dark roast coffee is more effective than light roast coffee in ... - NCBI." 2 Aug. 2018,
    https://www.ncbi.nlm.nih.gov/pubmed/21809439. Accessed 24 Jun. 2019.

9   "Coffee and cancer risk: a summary overview. - NCBI." https://www.ncbi.nlm.nih.
    gov/pubmed/28288025. Accessed 24 Jun. 2019.

10 "Effects of oral caffeine on postdural puncture headache. A ... - NCBI." https://www.
    ncbi.nlm.nih.gov/pubmed/2405733. Accessed 25 Jun. 2019.

11   "Systematic review of the potential adverse effects of caffeine ... - NCBI." 21 Apr. 2017, https://www.ncbi.nlm.nih.gov/pubmed/28438661. Accessed 25 Jun. 2019.

12   "Spilling the Beans: How Much Caffeine is Too Much? | FDA." 12 Dec. 2018, https://www.fda.gov/consumers/consumer-updates/spilling-beans-how-much-caffeine-too-much. Accessed 24 Jun. 2019.

13   "Effects of caffeine on human health. - NCBI." https://www.ncbi.nlm.nih.gov/pubmed/12519715. Accessed 24 Jun. 2019.

14   "The effects of a low dose of caffeine on cognitive performance. - NCBI." https://www.ncbi.nlm.nih.gov/pubmed/9862410. Accessed 25 Jun. 2019.

15   "The effects of black tea and other beverages on aspects of ... - NCBI." https://www.ncbi.nlm.nih.gov/pubmed/9784078. Accessed 25 Jun. 2019.

16   "Acute neurocognitive effects of epigallocatechin gallate (EGCG). - NCBI." 20 Nov. 2011, https://www.ncbi.nlm.nih.gov/pubmed/22127270. Accessed 26 Jun. 2019.

17   "Pharmacokinetics and safety of green tea polyphenols ... - NCBI - NIH." 15 Aug. 2003, https://www.ncbi.nlm.nih.gov/pubmed/12960117. Accessed 25 Jun. 2019.

18   "An intervention study on the effect of matcha tea, in drink and ... - NCBI." 5 May. 2017, https://www.ncbi.nlm.nih.gov/pubmed/28784536. Accessed 26 Jun. 2019.

19   "Stress-Reducing Function of Matcha Green Tea in Animal ... - NCBI." 10 Oct. 2018, https://www.ncbi.nlm.nih.gov/pubmed/30308973. Accessed 26 Jun. 2019.

20   "Yerba Mate Tea (Ilex paraguariensis): a comprehensive review - NCBI." https://www.ncbi.nlm.nih.gov/pubmed/18034743. Accessed 27 Jun. 2019.

21   "Consumption of yerba mate (Ilex paraguariensis) improves serum ..." https://www.ncbi.nlm.nih.gov/pubmed/19694438. Accessed 27 Jun. 2019.

22   "Maté consumption and risk of cancer: a multi-site case-control ... - NCBI." https://www.ncbi.nlm.nih.gov/pubmed/21790257. Accessed 27 Jun. 2019.

23   "A Double-Blind Placebo-Controlled Trial of Maca Root as Treatment ..." https://www.ncbi.nlm.nih.gov/pmc/articles/PMC4411442/. Accessed 27 Jun. 2019.

24   "Lepidium meyenii (Maca) improved semen parameters in adult men.." https://www.ncbi.nlm.nih.gov/pubmed/11753476. Accessed 27 Jun. 2019.

25   "Maca reduces blood pressure and depression, in a pilot study in ..." https://www.ncbi.nlm.nih.gov/pubmed/24931003. Accessed 27 Jun. 2019.

26   "Safety of Caffeine Usage - Caffeine for the Sustainment of ... - NCBI." https://www.ncbi.nlm.nih.gov/books/NBK223789/. Accessed 27 Jun. 2019.

27   "Caffeinism - Wikipedia." https://en.wikipedia.org/wiki/Caffeinism. Accessed 27 Jun. 2019.

28   "Caffeine fatalities--four case reports. - NCBI." https://www.ncbi.nlm.nih.gov/pubmed/14687776. Accessed 27 Jun. 2019.

29   "Safety of Caffeine Usage - Caffeine for the Sustainment of ... - NCBI." https://www.ncbi.nlm.nih.gov/books/NBK223789/. Accessed 27 Jun. 2019.

30   "Effects of caffeine on human health. - NCBI." https://www.ncbi.nlm.nih.gov/pubmed/12519715. Accessed 27 Jun. 2019.

CPSIA information can be obtained
at www.ICGtesting.com
Printed in the USA
BVHW040342010623
665165BV00004B/12